TWILIGHT OF EMPIRE:
Responses to Occupation

—

TWILIGHT OF EMPIRE: RESPONSES TO OCCUPATION

ISBN 978-0-9895616-8-6
© 2015 Perceval Press
© 2003, © 2005 Perceval Press
© 2003 All texts remain copyright of authors
© 2003 All images remain copyright of Lynsey Addario/Corbis

3rd edition

Published by Perceval Press
1223 Wilshire Blvd., Suite F
Santa Monica, CA 90403
www.percevalpress.com

"Seeking Honesty in U.S. Policy" by Joseph Wilson, reprinted with permission of the *San Jose Mercury News*.

"Stretched Thin, Lied to, and Mistreated" by Christian Parenti, reprinted
with permission of *The Nation*.

"Veiled and Worried in Baghdad" by Lauren Sandler, reprinted with permission of the *New York Times*.

"Every Morning the War Gets Up from Sleep," by Fadhil al-Azzawi,
reprinted with permission from the author and Boa Editions, Ltd.

Editors: Mark LeVine, Viggo Mortensen, Pilar Perez
Design: Michele Perez
Copy Editor: Sherri Schottlaender

Printed in Spain at Jomagar, S/A

Cover image: An American soldier from the First Cavalry Division
hits women with a stick as he tries to maintain order during a propane
distribution. LYNSEY ADDARIO/CORBIS 2003

TWILIGHT OF EMPIRE:
Responses to Occupation

PERCEVAL PRESS

CONTENTS

All photographs by Lynsey Addario

FOREWORD *to the twelfth anniversary edition*

The crimes against the people of Iraq documented in this important book continue to unfold. Iraq remains one of the most violent places on earth. Millions have been displaced. A cycle of sectarian violence encouraged — and institutionalized — by the United States is likely to play out for years to come. Women have seen hard-won social gains set back decades. All of this was predictable — and indeed was predicted — but ignored by an establishment press that paved the way for the invasion and occupation, and a political elite that spoke of democracy and freedom but was in truth guided by the vision of Condoleezza Rice, George Bush's national security adviser and later secretary of state. In the immediate aftermath of the September 11 attacks — which had nothing whatsoever to do with Iraq — Rice asked senior national security staff to think about how to "capitalize on these opportunities," which were "shifting the tectonic plates in international politics" to the advantage of the United States. "I really think this period is analogous to 1945 to 1947," she told Nicholas Lemann of the *New Yorker*. "And it's important to try to seize on that and position American interests and institutions and all of that before they harden again."

In reality, Washington has created greater instability throughout the region, seen its own influence diminished, enhanced the power of Iran, and spurred extremely reactionary religious and political currents, all at great cost to the people of Iraq and its neighbors. The devastation of Iraq started long before, when Washington actively backed and armed the brutal regime of Saddam Hussein as it carried out its worst abuses. It continued through years of sanctions that did not harm the regime, but stunted and killed the poor, elderly, and most vulnerable in Iraq. It was further exacerbated by years of aerial warfare against the country, foreshadowing the drone wars of today.

Instead of acknowledging these crimes — let alone paying reparations for them, as a small but principled wing of the antiwar movement has rightly demanded — the U.S. government and establishment press have spun new fictions to justify its past actions in Iraq and pave the way for renewed intervention. In this mythology, "we" (in the common phrasing of the media that so uncritically embrace rather than challenge our government) may have "lost our way" at certain points in Iraq, but then "the surge worked," a fiction that allowed the Bush administration to cover for its crimes in Iraq and, as Stephen M. Walt observed in *Foreign Policy*, "let President Bush hand the problem off to his successor." Then, just as we were securing the peace in Iraq, we pulled out prematurely and "abandoned" the country. Our failure, that is, was not the invasion and occupation but the withdrawal of most U.S. forces.

On national news programs today, the requirement for being an "expert" on any particular U.S. military action seems to be that you were wrong about Iraq. Should you have been right about Iraq's weapons of mass destruction and what U.S. intervention would mean for Iraq (and many, relying on history and commonsense, did predict the disaster to come), you are as likely to be asked to comment as ordinary

Iraqis themselves, whose silencing continues.

The antiwar movement did mobilize to prevent war against Iraq. A small number of people continued the work of organizing once that battle was lost, while so many others became demoralized and quit. But the movement was unable to survive the impact of the electoral turn of so many in the movement who saw in Illinois senator Barack Obama a chance for a break with the hated policies of the Bush administration. In reality, this was an illusion. Obama has continued and in many cases escalated Bush-era executive powers that give the president the authority to project power globally, engage in mass warrantless surveillance, violate civil liberties, kill "suspected terrorists" (including U.S. citizens) in a targeted assassination program that lacks any meaningful due process, and expand the use of deadly Special Operations kill teams. But the people who might have been in the streets and protesting these same actions under Bush now offer apologetics when they are carried out by Obama. In his two terms in office, Obama has more deeply entrenched these lethal programs, and will make it easier for any successor to expand them even further. As the *Guardian* reported in February 2015, "Barack Obama's proposed framework for the US-led war against the Islamic State will not restrict the battlefield to Iraq and Syria, multiple congressional sources said, ... placing the U.S. into a second simultaneous global war that will outlast his presidency." In addition, "Congressional language to retroactively justify the six-month-old US war against Isis will not, they said, scrap the broad 9/11–era authorities against al-Qaida, as some congressional Democrats had proposed, meaning that the two war authorizations will coexist. Asked if the anti-ISIS [Islamic State] AUMF [Authorization to Use Military Force] opens the U.S. to a second worldwide war against a nebulous adversary, one congressional aide answered: 'Absolutely.'"

Writing in the *New York Times Book Review* in January 2015, the author Mark Danner argued:

> On or about Sept. 11, 2001, American character changed. What Americans had proudly flaunted as "our highest values" were now judged to be luxuries that in a new time of peril the country could ill afford. Justice, and its cardinal principle of innocent until proven guilty, became a risk, its indulgence a weakness. Asked recently about an innocent man who had been tortured to death in an American "black site" in Afghanistan, former Vice President Dick Cheney did not hesitate. "I'm more concerned," he said, "with bad guys who got out ... than I am with a few that, in fact, were innocent." In this new era in which all would be sacrificed to protect the country, torture and even murder of the innocent must be counted simply "collateral damage."

But Danner is wrong. History matters. And this narrative, like so much discussion of Iraq, erases it. In fact, the U.S. government has long engaged in torture, carried out human rights abuses in the name of spreading its unique "values," showed its loudly proclaimed ideals to be ideological cover for its real motivations, and explained away any civilian casualties as "collateral damage." In fact, this imperial mindset is at the core of "American character."

However, there is another tradition in this country — one embodied in the speeches of Eugene Debs, the resistance of soldiers in Vietnam and Iraq, the strikes of dockworkers against the makers of armaments, the writings and example of Howard Zinn, and the people who contributed to *Twilight of Empire*. This is a tradition that sees itself firmly in solidarity with the people who live at the wrong end of the guns, cruise missiles, and drone strikes. It is also a tradition that understands that we have a special responsibility, as those who live within the empire, to work to systematically dismantle it. This is no longer an ethical or political question alone, but a question of survival of the species, since empire is at its root intimately connected with the drive toward economic domination that spurs conflict and war, as well as environmental destruction.

Anthony Arnove is on the editorial board of Haymarket Books and the *International Socialist Review*. He produced the Academy Award–nominated documentary *Dirty Wars* and wrote, directed, and produced *The People Speak* with Howard Zinn. He is the editor of several books, including *Voices of a People's History of the United States*, which Arnove co-edited with Zinn and was released in an updated tenth anniversary edition in 2014, *Howard Zinn Speaks*, *The Essential Chomsky*, and *Iraq Under Siege*, and is the author of *Iraq: The Logic of Withdrawal*.

PRECIPITATE PEACE

Those of us who knew in 2002 that there was no cause to invade Iraq, those who raised their voices for the cause of peace, who gathered together, marched, protested and lobbied incessantly against the unjustified rush to war, summoned the power of their humanity to demand that America's leaders cease and desist from their ill-considered plan to attack that Western Asian country. With the publication of *Twilight of Empire* 12 years ago, all who cared enough to challenge the venality and prevarication of the U.S. government could have seen that a benchmark had been established in chronicling the abject corruption of this unprovoked aggression.

Unfortunately, the will to war against Iraq was so powerful that it nullified the demands of millions of Americans who openly and vocally insisted Iraq should not be made to pay a price for the terrorist attacks of 9/11, which that country had nothing to do with. The will to war ignored all evidence brought forward in October of 2002 (and presented directly by myself to fellow Members of Congress), which posited that Iraq had nothing to do with 9/11, that Iraq had no intention or capability of attacking the U.S., and that Iraq did not have weapons of mass destruction.

An inversion of reality occurred, which claimed "absence of evidence is not evidence of absence." The media was reduced to being a spear-carrier for the government. Over 1,000,000 innocent Iraqis died as a result of the war, mass murder in the cradle of civilization. Hundreds of billions of dollars of damage was wreaked against a sovereign nation, whose society was consequently dismembered.

A form of philosophical anarchism has been inflicted on the American psyche: The laws of cause and effect have been suspended. We roam the world freely, often secretly, visiting wanton violence on masses of people, deny our actions, and then, when the oppressed lash back - or their sympathizers lash forward - we play the victim and demand retribution. We are in a closed loop of violent, covert attacks by the U.S., violent responses by those it attacks, subsequent U.S. counter attacks, more violent responses, and on and on. We must break this cycle or it will consume our nation.

The world's most powerful nation does not play the role of victim well. It does not suit our national character or our history. Nor does the fear which is filigreed into so many communications from the government to the media, to the people. Our social reality has been reconstructed, subverting the Constitution through lies and through the imposition of a permanent state of emergency, a national security state to make the American people compliant and faint-hearted in the face of rising fascism.

I saw all this happen from inside Congress. I spoke out. I was not alone. The pages of this book contain the testimony of others who knew, who recognised what was happening, who spoke out and objected, who stood for the truth.

If the truth shall free us, we are still waiting for deliverance. If lies imprison us, the self-forged bars which tie the tongue and still the will to act are being bent by those who have had the courage to call the war against Iraq what it was: wholesale murder in the name of the national security of the United States.

I cannot think of Iraq without deep passions stirring sentiments of terrible injustice. There must be accountability for those who took us into this unjustified war of aggression and occupation. The truth must be rescued from the scaffold of phony nationalism and false patriotism. The lies and the liars must be put on display. They must explain. They must repent. They must be made to atone. They must receive justice, as the people of Iraq have not.

We must repair the breach which the war created in Iraq. This is not simply a financial imperative, it is a moral imperative. A process of truth and reconciliation is urgently needed in the United States to free us from the duplicity which took us to war, and the ignorance which permits our US government to continue to wantonly pursue an American imperium, through militarism, unilateralism, pre-emptive strikes, endless coups, assassinations, and mayhem without end.

This is not the America we should tolerate. This is an America which is crying out for correction, a closing of the archipelago of military bases which encircle the globe, a cessation of fueling conflicts by sending US arms, often to parties in direct conflict with each other. It is time to redefine our national security in terms of jobs, decent wages, equal pay for men and women, housing, education, universal healthcare, retirement security, safe neighborhoods and freedom from government spying.

The government of the United States of America, with the compliance of the majority of its citizens, dragged Iraq into a slaughter house and emerged not only with the blood of Iraqi civilians and American soldiers on its hands, but having killed the hopes and aspirations of the American people as well. Trillions of dollars were wasted, our national debt spiraled, our infrastructure has fallen apart, our middle class has dwindled, our national purpose has been hijacked for the self-serving cause of war profiteers and vicious ideologues.

The world is at a turning point in human affairs. Either we will become attuned to the powerful rhythms of human unity which are the irresistible impulse of a world of social networking, interconnectedness and interdependence, or we will descend into a maelstrom of increasingly dangerous discontinuity, where, as Yeats wrote a century ago, "all things fall apart, the center cannot hold." I refuse to believe that the power of the human spirit which animated the foundation of a nation conceived in liberty cannot now re-conceptualize itself, reform and rededicate the United States of America in the common cause of humanity, in order to not simply survive war, but to thrive in peace.

We must now precipitate peace as eagerly as we precipitated war. We must work to achieve for the United States a benevolent role in the world as a nation among nations, working with the global community on matters of human security. We cannot achieve a new condition, however, unless we are prepared to begin the difficult work of examining the conduct of those who led us into the Iraq war, and the consequences of that war.

The *Twilight of Empire* marked a beginning in this process of self-examination as regards the cause and effects of this war. How far we are prepared to travel with its information will be a test of how much we truly love our nation.

EDITOR'S NOTE 2015

Our instincts lead us to search for permanence, for clear markers to gauge where we've come from, who we are, and what our place and part might be in the events taking place in our homes and around the world. The pursuit of something concrete, reliable, and quantifiable is the foundation of philosophy, and, often, the manifestation of a need to feel sane in an unpredictable world. Sometimes this drive to feel we know how things stand, for specific information to base our likes and dislikes on, leads us to fabricate enemies in a very primitive way, to develop "us against them" scenarios that might give us a sense of purpose and affiliation, not to mention personal exculpation. "Who is the bad guy?", I or you often ask, consciously and unconsciously, assuming it cannot be us. As Noam Chomsky once said, "Everybody's worried about stopping terrorism. Well, there's a really easy way: stop participating in it". This book attempted, twelve years ago, to deal with facts leading up to and following the U.S.-led invasion and occupation of Iraq. With the benefit of hindsight, we can re-read these first-hand accounts and analyses of that time and understand not only how subsequent foreign policy decisions have served to exacerbate a terrible situation, but how, to varying degrees, each one of us has been, inadvertently or not, complicit in the ongoing debacle. Lessons from then and for now in an ongoing examination of the facts as each of us chooses to perceive them.

Viggo Mortensen,
Perceval Press
May, 2015

An American soldier from the First Cavalry Division hits women with a stick as he tries to maintain order during a propane distribution. LYNSEY ADDARIO/CORBIS 2003

The more progress we make on the ground, the more free Iraqis become, the more electricity is available, the more jobs are available, the more kids that are going to school, the more desperate these killers become because they can't stand the thought of a free society.
—President George W. Bush

This is the first time that I have seen a parallel to Vietnam, in terms of information that the administration is putting out versus the actual situation on the ground.
—Senator John McCain

The glaring contradiction between "the actual situation on the ground" and what often seems to be a deliberately misleading picture painted for public consumption by the Bush administration has created an informational void that a largely cajoled and co-opted mainstream media has shown little or no interest in filling. The dangerous gap between what we are told and what can readily be observed in places like U.S.-occupied Iraq and Afghanistan makes the firsthand information and reasoned assessments offered in books like this one indispensable.

While *Twilight of Empire: Responses to Occupation* does not claim to provide an exhaustive overview of motivations for, or consequences of recent U.S.-led invasions and occupations, it does provide significant new pieces of the evolving puzzle. If "truth is found where contradictions meet," as writer Lindsay Clarke put it, then this book can serve to guide those who would try to find that meeting place. It is, in fact, dedicated to all people, whether they be from the United States, Afghanistan, Iraq, or elsewhere, who strive to keep an open mind and work for peace.

V.M.,
Perceval Press
2003

Haitham Hashim, 26, a police officer in the Kazimiya Police force, holds a girl's sandal that he found amidst the destruction of an explosion in Baghdad. LYNSEY ADDARIO/CORBIS 2004

PREVIOUS SPREAD: An Iraqi woman walks through a plume of smoke rising from a massive fire at a liquid gas factory as she searches for her husband in the vicinity of the fire in Basra. LYNSEY ADDARIO/CORBIS 2003

FOREWORD *to the second edition*

It has been a year since *Twilight of Empire* was first published, with its extraordinary collection of firsthand accounts, incisive essays, and poetry presenting the war in Iraq with a vivid intensity rarely matched in the literature on that war. Tragically, the picture it presented of Iraq under United States occupation has not changed—it is in fact reinforced by what we read in news accounts every day.

As I write this in the fall of 2004, the number of dead U.S. soldiers has exceeded one thousand, and every day there are more killed and wounded. When Medea Benjamin wrote from Baghdad in early 2003 that "the clock is ticking and patience is wearing thin," she was describing a phenomenon applicable to both Americans and Iraqis, who are still enduring death and suffering long after President Bush triumphantly declared "Mission Accomplished."

The Bush Administration has made strenuous attempts to conceal from the public photos of bodies being returned to the U.S., as well as information about the thousands of wounded soldiers. Nevertheless, those stories have emerged, even if only sporadically, in the mainstream press. A story in the *New York Times* on December 30, 2003, told of a young man who, after months in Iraq, came home blinded. His mother, visiting him in the hospital, saw a young female soldier crawling along the floor, her legs gone, her three-year-old son trailing behind her.

On September 22, 2004, war correspondent Chris Hedges related the story of Sue Niederer, whose only son had been killed in Iraq: Niederer showed up at a Republican gathering in her New Jersey town to confront Laura Bush with a sign that read, "President Bush killed my son," and shouting, "Why don't your children serve?" She was arrested and handcuffed before being released.

Sue Niederer's outburst is a reflection of an increasing anger against the war among families who have lost loved ones. Another mother, Ruth Aitken, whose son was killed in fighting around Baghdad, told a reporter, "It makes me mad that this whole war was sold to the American public and to the soldier as something it wasn't." A number of these outraged parents have formed a group called Military Families Against the War. One of the group's leading members is the father of Marine Lance Corporal Jesus Suarez del Solar, who has said that his son died for "Bush's oil."

Although the casualty toll among U.S. soldiers has been played down by the government and has not been emphasized by the media, the grim news nevertheless has eroded the public's patience with the war. By mid-2004 polls showed that more than half of the American people felt that the war is not worth its cost in human suffering.

The word "impatience" is wholly inadequate to describe the Iraqi reaction to the U.S. military presence. Profound sadness at the fate of their country, grief at the death of family and friends, fury at the occupiers—those are the dominant reactions of the Iraqi people as reported by observers on the ground. As an example, Jodie Evans quotes an Iraqi in this volume: "Are the Americans doing this to destroy us?"

The Iraqi victims of this war have been largely invisible in the American press, which has obsequiously followed the lead of the Pentagon. The Pentagon itself says again and again that it does not keep track of Iraqi casualties. I recall the statement of General Colin Powell at the end of the first Gulf War in 1991, when he boasted about the small number of U.S. casualties; when asked about Iraqi casualties in this war, he replied, "That is a matter I am not terribly concerned with."

Also in this book, Kristina Borjesson, an independent journalist, speaking with her interviewer about the control of information on American television, states that the reality of human suffering is hidden from the public. As I write this in September of 2004, a Knight Ridder report of statistics compiled by the Iraqi health ministry (like other Iraqi ministries, it is under the authority of the occupying forces) says that in just the five previous months, 3,487 Iraqis have died, most of them civilians, and many of them children.

Statistics, no matter how shocking, are cold and inadequate. In the same news report, Dr. Mumtz Jaber, a vascular surgeon in Baghdad, told of his sister and brother-in-law, who did not stop fast enough at an American checkpoint; their three-year-old son was shot and killed when soldiers opened fire. At the morgue in Baghdad, the physician there said he saw a family of eight brought in—three women, three men, two children—who were sleeping on their roof (it was too hot inside) when a military helicopter shot and killed them all.

One would have to multiply such individual stories by the thousands to grasp the reality of a military operation that claims only to be fighting against "terrorists." You will find in this book, in the piece by journalist Eman Ahmed Khammas, a Sunni Muslim who lives in Baghdad, figures from Iraq Body Count. This group of British and U.S. researchers reports that during the war (that is, in the several weeks of "shock and awe" before the occupation itself) close to 8,000 Iraqis were killed, with 20,000 injured.

And what of those Iraqis—perhaps 10,000 or more—who have been seized from their homes or off the streets to be put into indefinite detention, simply on "suspicion," with no hearings, no right to attorneys, no charges filed. Some of these people will be released months later, without any explanation. The treatment suffered by these detainees may range from ordinary humiliation to the sexual abuse and torture inflicted by U.S. forces in Abu Ghraib prison.

A February 2004 report by the International Committee of the Red Cross (ICRC) said about these detainees: "In almost all instances . . . arresting authorities provided no information about who they were . . . nor did they explain the cause of arrest. . . . Certain military intelligence officers told the ICRC that in their estimate, between 80 percent and 90 percent of the persons deprived of their liberty in Iraq had been arrested by mistake."

And what about the lives of those Iraqis who escape death, mutilation, or imprisonment? How do they live day by day? They live, for the most part, without clean water or electricity or adequate health care or sewage disposal, and they live in a state of constant fear. What the U.S. government has called the "reconstruction" of Iraq has become a sorry joke—it is really a story of profiteering and corruption. A Reuters dispatch in August 2004 reported that an official U.S. audit found that more than $8 billion given to Iraqi ministries by the former U.S.-led authority could not be accounted for.

Naomi Klein's piece in this volume provides a clue to the reasons for this disaster: the U.S. government, with its utter devotion to the capitalist ethic of greed, has in effect turned the Iraqi economy over to multinational corporations who have swarmed all over the country with only one thought in mind—profit. When the profit motive is primary, human needs are left behind.

Klein finds in Iraq a microcosm of what has been happening all over the world—the power of the United States and the World Bank and the International Monetary Fund has been used to turn public enterprises over to private corporations, and this insistence on deregulation has had calamitous results for ordinary people. While the press shows photos of poor people looting stores, Klein gives us a larger picture, revealing the "economic looting" of Iraq by the multinationals.

Perhaps it's no wonder that someone has painted the following phrase in English under the new statue that has replaced the dismantled statue of Saddam Hussein in Baghdad: "All done. Go home."

It is refreshing to find in the pages of this book the thoughts and the feelings of Muslims opposed to the American occupation who believe in nonviolent solutions. Americans need to be acquainted with such sentiments in order to reject the ideas put forth by some intellectuals in the United States who speak about "Muslim fanaticism" and a "clash of civilizations."

I have no doubt that the reason so many Americans still support the Iraq war is that they remain mostly ignorant of history due to what Studs Terkel has called "our national amnesia." This ignorance begins in school and is perpetuated by the mass media and the political leadership of the nation. If there were some sense of history among Americans, they would immediately connect the word "occupation" with the second World War, when we became familiar with the phrases "occupied France," "occupied Denmark," "occupied Europe." The word "occupation" suggests a shocking connection between Hitler's invasion of other countries—he also claimed to "liberating" them—and the unprovoked U.S. invasion of Iraq. And then, perhaps recalling the "resistance movements" in France and elsewhere in Europe, people might begin to understand why the Iraqis are violently resisting the American presence in their country.

Most Americans do not know the history of the Middle East, and Mike Davis reminds us in these pages about the brutal British conquest of the very same lands now occupied by American and British forces. Does Prime Minister Tony Blair not feel a twinge of shame at the thought that he is engaging in a pitiful re-creation of those years after World War I when English planes bombed helpless villagers and Winston Churchill proposed the use of poison gas against the resisting Arabs? Davis reminds us that the "aerial terror" tactics we have become accustomed to since Ethiopia, the Spanish Civil War, and World War II—since Addis Ababa, Madrid, Dresden, Tokyo, Hiroshima, Nagasaki—began in the Middle East with the bombing of Libya. And yes, the British Empire was "victorious," but at what horrific cost to the people of in the region? And did that victory not end ultimately in ignominy?

Is that not the fate of arrogant empires, and will that not be our own fate, sooner or later? Have we forgotten that in Vietnam, the longest of American wars, even with our enormous, frightening military machine with its B-52 bombers, its chemical weapons, its unsurpassed technology, we eventually had to exit that destroyed land even as our leaders insisted all the while that we must "stay the course?"

Books like this one help spread the truth, which has a power greater than guns. Empires topple because human beings can only take so much of tyranny, whether it comes from inside or from abroad. Through all the haze of violence and suffering, we may be seeing the twilight of empire.

An Iraqi man detained by soldiers with the 4th Infantry Division, 3rd Brigade, from the 1st Battalion–68th Armored Regiment, stands bound against a wall in a compound. LYNSEY ADDARIO/CORBIS 2003

INTRODUCTION

Twilight of Empire: Responses to Occupation offers an incisive and moving collection of perspectives in these increasingly dangerous times. Written at a moment when a president who was not popularly elected is declaring endless war, the essays, interviews, and reports in this book are each a critical piece of the arguments that need to be heard now more than ever.

On September 11, 2001, we were broadcasting *Democracy Now!* from our studio in the garret of a nineteenth-century firehouse in New York City's Chinatown. Blocks away, the first jet had hit the north tower of the World Trade Center. At 9:03 A.M., the second plane hit the second tower. We heard a faint boom, but from within our studios it sounded like a common sound of the city. We soon got word of the horror and destruction that was occurring just blocks away from us at what was to become known as Ground Zero. We finished the show but kept our line open to the satellite uplink at Pacifica station KPFA in Berkeley, and we continued broadcasting throughout the day. Our colleagues at Downtown Community Television, the non-profit television production and training facility that owns the firehouse, opened the doors and offered the people streaming up the road water and use of telephones. We brought people upstairs to broadcast their eyewitness accounts. At 5 P.M. we witnessed the collapse of Building Seven, most likely as a result of Rudolph Giuliani's ill-placed Emergency Command Center's massive diesel fuel depot within.

An evacuation zone was established at Canal Street, two blocks to the north of us, so the *Democracy Now!* crew decided to stay in the firehouse so we could continue to broadcast over the coming days. We slept on the floor for three nights as the military occupied Lower Manhattan. Early in the morning of Friday, September 14, I went out with another *Democracy Now!* producer, and we walked toward Ground Zero. The streets were empty: buildings and abandoned cars were completely covered with dust that has since been proven to be highly toxic. There were Humvees and portable klieg lights closer to Ground Zero, parked at intersections filled with pallets of bottled water and exhausted-looking members of the National Guard. As we navigated as close as we could, we witnessed the smoldering ruins, saw the fires still raging undergound, and watched the heavy traffic of trucks hauling away load after load of steel beams piled like fallen logs.

Turned back at a security gate, we rounded back to Church Street, past Wall Street, and on to Battery Park, at Manhattan's southernmost tip, which had become a bustling military camp. Olive-green vehicles of all sizes circled the park. Signs had been hung with billeting instructions and security detachment schedules, all in the military's inscrutable jargon. It was still hours before dawn, but hundreds were awake and at work. We encountered a woman in green camouflage fatigues. She was from upstate New York and was a helicopter pilot in the National Guard. We asked her what she thought. She had just arrived and was likely going to be assigned to guard duty, protecting access to Ground Zero. She said that she was horrified at the scene of devastation a block away. She then said something that was both unexpected, but not altogether surprising: she said she hoped that there wouldn't be a military response, that as a mother she didn't want to see more death come out of this act of terrorism. She declined to speak on camera, even anonymously, but her words stayed with me.

Soon after, the Bush administration announced the color-coded Terror Alert System, with colors designating the government's publicly pronounced assessment of the threat of a terrorist attack. Since that time, all of New York City has remained on Orange Alert, with green-camouflaged soldiers from the National Guard with machine guns at the ready standing out amidst the white paint and concrete of our subway stations. NYPD Commandos in body armor, also with machine guns, patrol the sidewalks and Starbucks of Manhattan. President Bush appointed Tom Ridge, the governor of Pennsylvania, to be the Secretary of Homeland Security: he created havoc nationally by encouraging people to cover their windows with plastic sheeting and duct tape.

In response to this color scheme—widely held to be a convenient public relations tool to manipulate people with fear when the Bush administration needed to distract the public from genuine issues—a group of women got together and formed Code Pink: Women for Peace. Bedecked in brilliant pink clothing, with pink feather boas and pink umbrellas, these women started networking to oppose war and to unify people against the use of 9/11 for cynical political goals. They protested, they maintained a continuous vigil outside the White House, and they networked through traditional means and via the Internet.

The global peace movement was unable to prevent the bombing of Afghanistan, in which thousands of civilians were killed—these deaths were referred to collectively by the Pentagon and their supportive press corps as "collateral damage." As U.S. Secretary of State Colin Powell says, "We don't count enemy dead." And so it was up to civil society, to journalists and activists from Code Pink and allied organizations, to go to Afghanistan and investigate and document the civilian casualties of the U.S.-led invasion. The stories were horrible and common: entire extended families were wiped out; U.S. helicopter gunships hovered over villages with no connection to the Taliban government or Al-Qaeda and rained bullets down on women and children. At *Democracy Now!* we followed these delegations, kept in touch with independent journalists like Robert Fisk and John Pilger, and broadcast this different picture of a bloody invasion that was ignored by the mainstream media.

By September 2002, with Osama bin Laden still at large and U.S. corporations enmeshed in an accelerating cascade of corporate scandals, the Bush administration, facing its most serious criticisms since 9/11, seemed strangely quiet. We were soon to find out why. I was just about to speak at the Power to the Peaceful Rally in San Francisco, organized by the great hip-hop artist Michael Franti, when Code Pink co-founder Medea Benjamin came over to me. "Did you hear what Andrew Card just said?" she asked. (Andrew Card is George W. Bush's Chief of Staff, and the former chief lobbyist for General Motors.) "From a marketing standpoint, you don't roll out a new product in August," Card said. Bush was just finishing up one of his many vacations, waiting for the proper moment to launch his new fall line with Tony Blair. On September 7, the two men held a joint press conference at Camp David and announced that Saddam Hussein was an imminent threat to the safety of the U.S. and Britain.

Thus began the six-month marketing blitz that led to the massive and violent implementation of the Bush Doctrine of preemptive war, with the now sadly familiar consequences: uncountable civilian casualties and continually mounting U.S. troop casualties. The occupation is causing a deepening crisis for the president and the British prime minister as it becomes costly, violent, and unpopular in Iraq and at home, even as the stated reasons for war remain unproven and have essentially been cast aside. At the time of this writing, more than 164,000 members of the National Guard and military reservists are on active duty, the majority of them having had their assignments lengthened. What for many soldiers was likely a way to supplement family income—as suggested in the recruitment slogan of "One weekend a month and two weeks a year"—has now become a living hell as they are stationed in cramped quarters in Iraq, in 120-degree weather, facing dangerous assignments and daily attacks from an invisible enemy.

The administration's chief weapons inspector, David Kay, returned from three months in Iraq with 1,200 inspectors, having spent $300 million. Number of weapons of mass destruction found: zero. He claims he needs $600 million more and asks for an additional six to nine more months. The timeline is not lost on anyone watching the presidential election cycle. The Republican Party very carefully chose New York as its convention city; the gathering will take place one week before September 11, 2004, and most regard this as both a grotesque politicization of the mass murder that occurred at Ground Zero and another carefully orchestrated rollout of a new product timed to coincide with the presidential campaign season.

With so much at stake, we each must take responsibility for the health of our democracy. We must hold those in power accountable, and we need to pressure the media to do its job of challenging those in power rather than acting as their stenographers. We need a society in which dissent is commonplace, so that when someone at work takes a break by the water cooler and hears someone else criticize those in power, it is not shocking. The major media in the U.S. must also be held accountable. It is not only Pacifica Radio, NPR, and PBS that use the public airwaves: ABC, CBS, and NBC all use them as well, and they are required by law to serve the public interest, which they fail to do with increasing audacity.

For the water-cooler dissenters, or for the many millions who once supported the government's actions but now have serious questions, this book will serve as an invaluable resource. Its pages are filled with eloquent firsthand accounts, reports from award-winning journalists, and expert analysis from people who are virtually excluded from the narrowly defined sound-bite exchanges that the mainstream media allow on their infotainment news programs.

Read this book, share this book, and engage in informed and frequent discussion on the topics within: Empire, Occupation, War, Peace. Regardless of your position on the issues, make debate and dissent commonplace, for debate and dissent are at the core of any strong, healthy democracy. Together we can break the sound barrier.

BAGHDAD JOURNAL #1

Medea Benjamin and I brought a group of fourteen people to Iraq in February 2003. About six months before that we had founded Code Pink: Women for Peace, a response to the Bush Administration's color-coded terrorist weather watch. Code Pink called on women and men to "wage peace" through proactive, creative protest and nonviolent direct action. Our February visit to Iraq was intended as a "preemptive strike" for peace—specifically, we tried to establish person-to-person contacts with Iraqi women and also report on what we saw and heard without the filter of corporate media. We returned to Iraq in July to witness the occupation.

"Is it better before or after the invasion?" I ask Faruk, who had cared for us so generously on our first trip to Baghdad in February.

"It was better during the bombing," he explains, with a look that says, can't you see for yourself? Later I learn that his house was bombed and he was still in the process of fixing it.

"Before, we had one Saddam. Now we have one hundred. Are the Americans doing this to destroy us?"

How can I answer this question? It is similar to the question I was asked during my February visit: "Why does Mr. Bush want to bomb us?"

In the aftermath of the U.S. invasion, we felt the need to return to Baghdad. We needed to see the people we had met on our previous trip, friends we thought of daily as we watched the fire and smoke of "shock and awe." We needed to learn how they had fared through the American invasion. We had also received funding and support to lay the groundwork for setting up the International Occupation Watch Center (IOWC), a project of United for Peace and Justice and a coalition of other international peace groups. The IOWC is intended to be an independent organization that will monitor the activities of the coalition military forces and foreign corporations, thus providing the international community with reliable, independent information; the IOWC also supports local efforts to improve the lives of the Iraqi people in order to help them rebuild their country and move toward self-rule.

Our delegation consisted of me, Reverend Patricia Ackerman, and Gael Murphy, all from Code Pink; Medea Benjamin of Global Exchange, the co-founder of Code Pink; Ted Lewis of Global Exchange; and documentary filmmakers Gerard Ungerman and Audrey Brohy.

As before, we flew to Amman, Jordan, to arrange the overland caravan crossing to Baghdad. In February the trip across the desert cost us 39 U.S. dollars; now the bidding was between $150 and $500. We settled on $175—as I wondered if the extra $25 would save us from the dangers on the road, I knew in my gut that it didn't really matter. We'd already surrendered to the fates in deciding to come here.

One encounters "Ali Baba" crime—a description used by Iraqis—when trying to cross the desert from Amman to Baghdad. About twenty cars a day are held up going through Fallouja, though the "Ali Babas" do let the occupants live. Actually, a GI at the border told us that these Ali Babas were kind, in general: last week they had taken a truck and all its contents but left the Jordanian driver by the side of the road with thirty dollars and his shirt so that he wouldn't be totally stranded.

To cross the desert and make the border in time for the caravan, we left our hotel at 1:30 in the morning. By the time we reached the border, the intense rose light of dawn spread across the desert. On the Jordanian side, hundreds of trucks waited to cross over, laden with merchandise of all sorts: packaged goods, computers, tires, plywood, machine parts, replacements for things either worn out from years of sanctions, destroyed in the bombing, or carried off by looters; most of this material is intended for the use of the occupying forces, because most Iraqis are without jobs or the money for such things. We met two Jordanians who were taking in a load of beer and alcohol. On our February trip it had been impossible to find a drink except in the high-rent district of Baghdad. Later, in Baghdad I would see drunken men roaming the streets, something I had never encountered before the war.

Some borders make sense, at least in terms of geography. The Jordanian side is relatively cool, with rolling hills and even evergreen trees. Crossing into Iraq one enters the desert, a vast, empty scrub done in various shades of dirt which goes on forever, unbroken save for the occasional little clump of cement-block buildings that constitute the villages in this region. The heat is all-encompassing, inescapable, filtered through the gray dust that hangs in the air and coats every surface. You are almost always thirsty, and everyone obsesses about water: where to get it, how much to carry.

It had taken three hours to enter Iraq in February—now it took minutes. We saw our first mutilated image of Saddam, its tiles scratched and gouged. A GI sat atop his dusty tank looking hot and bored, like all the other GIs around the border, their guns strapped to their legs and machine guns thrown over their shoulders.

We were conducted to a cinderblock structure built on a cement slab, a contrast to the inviting and comfortable living room where we'd been greeted in February and taught a few words of Arabic as we were served chai.

"That sucks!" someone shouted as we entered the small room.

The speaker was a young GI from Colorado named Rick, who was not much more than eighteen years old. He was visibly distraught, jittery, pacing around the bare dirty room as if his body could not contain his nerves. He could not seem to stop talking. Another slightly older GI sat silently in a corner, his face expressionless, a machine gun on his lap.

We gave our passports to the bored Iraqi man behind the window. He barely looked at our documents as he stamped them (no visas required)—we could have been anyone. Paul Bremer declared that with the exception of weapons and drugs, anything could be brought into the country, duty-free, for a period of three months; though we could have been smuggling kilos of heroin and Uzis, no one bothered to open our bags.

Anyone, it seemed, could now get into Iraq, and everyone was: Jordanians, Palestinians, all coming in waves from the surrounding Arab countries. There were businessmen from Europe and Japan in silly-looking black suits, and American men from the South. All were looking to profit from the new Wild West, the Iraqi Gold Rush, where there are few rules and little authority to get in the way of profits.

Heaps of trash and sewage line the streets of Baghdad. LYNSEY ADDARIO/CORBIS 2003

Our friend Amal would tell us later as we sat in her garden: "We are a wounded animal in the forest; everyone is coming to take their piece of our flesh."

After the perfunctory ritual of having our passports stamped, we talked a while with the GIs stationed in the room. The younger of the two, the anxious eighteen-year-old from Colorado, was upset because he had tried to call his girlfriend on a cell phone borrowed from a Danish businessman, and just as he had finally made the connection, the phone died. He hadn't spoken to her in more than a month, and he was sure she was about to dump him. "She's gonna leave me," he repeated, "I know she's gonna: I'm gonna get that Dear John letter, I can tell"—that is, when the mail finally arrived. The soldiers'

living conditions, we quickly discovered, were miserable: erratic mail, bad meals, uncomfortable beds, hellish heat, and no idea when they'd be going home.

"You missed the caravan," Rick informed us. "They took off a half hour ago." He suggested that we wait for another but had no idea when that might be. A look of concern crossed his face when we voted to go it alone.

Hassan, our driver, wasn't too concerned. "Don't worry," he told us. "Before we get to Fallouja, I will stop at my friend's grocery store and pick up a machine gun. We'll put it in the middle of the front seat and the Ali Babas won't bother us."

The road out from the border crossing area is gone; we have to make our way across the desert. Looking to the side we see a crater of concrete and steel ripped and peeled back by a missile. It reminds Patricia and me of Amriya, the bomb shelter we visited in February where more than four hundred women and children were killed by American missiles in 1991. A thick silence filled the car.

Our six-hour drive through "Ali Baba land" (our driver's expression) was uneventful. We sped down the highway past the debris of battle: the carcasses of tanks, Humvees, overturned buses, exploded shells, and bomb craters, along with the occasional shepherd and his flock picking their way through the rubble.

We passed the skeleton of a burnt-out red Ferrari.

"Uday's," our driver informed us.

I have no way of knowing if that was true or not, and I don't think it matters. It's the truth that people tell themselves, the story that they've created to make some sense of the chaos: Here is the wreckage of Uday's Ferrari, the ruined remains of Saddam's regime.

The Baghdad that greeted us in July was not the Baghdad we'd left in February. Most of the taller buildings have been destroyed or damaged, leaving crumpled steel frames, burnt-out shells, walls full of holes and scarred by flames. Rolls of razor wire lined the streets. The air was a haze of dust weighed down by heat. As we crossed the bridge that leads to the street where our apartment was, we could see the destruction along the banks of the Tigris, where nearly every building appeared to be damaged. The United Nations Development Program was an empty husk with black scorch marks rising from the windows, as if the flames had left their shadows behind. On the Tigris side, all the restaurants were abandoned and wrecked, either from the bombing or the looting.

Tanks blocked opposing traffic about halfway to our hotel, so cars came straight at us as they made left turns; we were salmon swimming upstream against the current of cars, with no traffic lights or controls of any sort. This was our first experience of life without electricity.

Earlier we had passed long lines of parked cars as we drove through the streets; we later learned that they were waiting for gas. Without electricity, the gas pumps don't work properly. To avoid the lines, some men arrive on foot with cans to fill by hand. Similar lines exist for kerosene and gas for cooking, because the gas isn't being delivered to people's homes. All of this has created a very dangerous situation. The hospitals are full of burn cases.

We again stayed in the Andaluz Apartments, across the street from the Palestine Hotel, where the Al-Jazeera reporter was killed by American tank fire. The owners and staff greeted us with hugs and celebration. We had all grown close during the tense days of our February stay, and it was a great relief to find that our friends had made it through the bombing. The staff of the Andaluz Apartments is in many ways typical of places that service foreigners: they are, in general, highly educated professionals who speak excellent English; many were engineers and English literature majors. They are doing jobs for which they are overqualified, but in a country under sanctions, the jobs for which they were trained frequently do not exist, and positions involving interaction with foreigners provide higher salaries and good tips.

Continued . . .

A U.S. soldier stands guard as a building burns behind him following a grenade attack on a Humvee in August 2003. LYNSEY ADDARIO/CORBIS 2003

THE UNGRATEFUL VOLCANO

Does the Pentagon have a "bureau of history"? Is there a room somewhere in that vast labyrinth where monkish researchers toil over the ancient archives of power, exhuming the lessons of colonies won and lost, empires risen and fallen?

I doubt it. The Pentagon's interest in history is probably the same as the Swiss passion for surfing or the Saudi Arabian enthusiasm for ice hockey: rather oxymoronic.

Too bad. A great deal of carnage might have been avoided if Donald Rumsfeld—or for that matter, Tony Blair—had bothered to read the letters of Gertrude Bell and the diaries of Winston Churchill. Gertie and Winnie knew the land between the rivers terribly well. After all, they were the ones who transformed three prosperous and ethnically distinct provinces of the Ottoman empire into an unhappy British client state.

"Iraq?" Been there and done it, old boy. Our turn was bloody tragedy; now you Yanks get the apocalyptic farce. Odd how history repeats itself on the banks of the Euphrates, isn't it? Cheerio.

Let us imagine what kind of memo these old imperials might have passed along to their cowboy descendants, a precis, as it were, of the previous occupation.

It wouldn't really be a "cautionary tale"—after all, we are already far too far up river in the heart of darkness. Caution and humanity have already been stuffed into body bags. But the British precedent might indicate a general trajectory for imperial hubris. They too started out expecting hugs and kisses and ended up giving back bombs and genocide.

1. MISS BELL'S TEA PARTY

What Woodrow Wilson would later denounce as the "whole disgusting scramble" for the Middle East began when the British invaded "Mesopotamia" in 1914. The War Office already knew that the twentieth century would be powered by petroleum, and officially the British were only protecting their oil properties in neighboring Persia from untoward Turkish or German attentions; unofficially, they were also prospecting for oil around Basra.

The conquest of Mesopotamia was supposed to be a triumphal procession in the face of desultory Turkish resistance. In actuality, it was a singularly unhappy hike that involved a lot of heat, dust, thirst, and dying. The British advance first turned into an ignominious retreat, and then a catastrophe at Kut-al-Amara in 1916. The British were forced to organize a second, far larger expedition. In 1917 the redcoats finally fought their way into Baghdad and allowed Miss Bell to take her tea on the banks of the Tigris.

The general presumption was that now that the bad Turks were gone, the rest of the population would shower love upon the British. "It's a wonderful thing to feel the affection and confidence of a whole people around you," Bell enthused in the early months of the occupation. Officially the Oriental Secretary (that is to say, the resident expert on the "Arab mind") in the British administration, the erudite and adventurous Miss Bell was Paul Wolfowitz *avant l'lettre:* the optimistic ideologue of the happy occupation.

Her blueprint was not dissimilar to the plan unveiled by the United States Deputy Secretary of Defense in winter 2003. The occupation of Iraq, according to Bell, would be strictly pay-as-you-go, with oil exploration—now doubled with the illegal British annexation in 1918 of the Mosul region—reimbursing the hard-pressed Exchequer, while Iraqis (although they were not yet called that) policed themselves under British supervision. Liberated from the iron heel of Ottoman rule, the locals would be slowly tutored in democratic values, even though the new dispensation was, in fact, based on arrogant English sahibs ruling in partnership with a handful of Sunni notables while Kurdish sheiks were arrested, Shia clerics persecuted, and tribal oil lands confiscated.

The population drew unfavorable comparisons between Turkish rule, with its comfortable quotient of local self-government, and British occupation, with its ruthless drive for efficiency, especially in the collection of taxes. Despite growing restiveness, Miss Bell was still camped on a cloud. "On the whole," she wrote in 1918, "the country is being opened up, and on the whole the people like it. . . . Basra is under peace conditions, and we have had almost no trouble in Baghdad." Her boss and Paul Bremer's predecessor, Sir Arnold Wilson, was equally optimistic: "The average Arab, as opposed to the handful of amateur politicians of Baghdad, sees the future as one of fair dealing and material and moral progress under the aegis of GB [Great Britain]."

The next year at Versailles, the broader Arab national cause—in whose service Bell and her colleague, Colonel T. E. Lawrence, had insinuated themselves early in the war—was comprehensively betrayed by the Anglo-French division of the Middle East which gave Zionism its beachhead in Palestine and turned Syria over to France. Mesopotamia, meanwhile, was the object of a fierce intramural struggle inside the government of Lloyd George. On one side were the "Indianists," who wanted an old-fashioned colony with lots of permanent sinecures for unemployed British aristocrats; on the other side were "Arabists" like Bell, who desperately wanted a throne to assuage the Hashemite dynasty just evicted by the Foreign Legion in Damascus. ("You will understand," one British official wrote to another, "that what is wanted is a King who will be content to reign but not govern.")

There was little concern about what the ordinary population thought about colonial satraps or foreign monarchs. The Kurds were especially impatient, and in May 1919 they rose up against the British and were crushed. Bell and others in Baghdad thought that was the end of the affair, while in London those in power were more worried about the Americans and Standard Oil's demands for a piece of Mesopotamia.

2. THE CHURCHILL DOCTRINE

At the same time, some of the most brilliant minds in London were concentrating on how to reduce the soaring costs of the occupation. Winston Churchill, who was both Secretary of State for War and for Air, wrote to Royal Air Force head Hugh Trenchard in February 1920 wondering if Britain couldn't economize by replacing troops with planes. He expressed interest in chemical weapons, like the mustard gas bombs that the RAF had used against the Bolsheviks. Trenchard was enthusiastic, and in March he responded with a detailed plan for air force control of Mesopotamia. It came just in time.

On May Day 1920, the Treaty of San Remo established Iraq as a British

Mandate. Three weeks later, four British soldiers were killed at Tel Afar, near Mosul, after the arrest of a local sheik. An armored car squadron was dispatched to restore order but was ambushed and annihilated by local rebels. It was the beginning of a general uprising—such as the United States may yet face—by Miss Bell's "affectionate" subjects.

Later Churchill would cynically marvel in private over his government's success in uniting the Iraqis against them. "It is an extraordinary thing that the British civil administration should have succeeded in such a short time in alienating the whole country to such an extent that the Arabs have laid aside the blood feuds they have nursed for centuries and that the Suni [sic] and Shiah [sic] tribes are working together. We have been advised locally that the best way to get our supplies up the river would be to fly the Turkish flag. . . ."

The leadership of the rebellion was drawn both from the purged cadre of the old regime (ex-Ottoman officers and officials) and from the angry Shia majority in the south. (Sound familiar?) By the middle of July fighting had spread throughout the lower Euphrates. Brigadier Coningham lost thirty-five men storming the insurgent citadel of Rumaitha only to find that rebels had moved on to seize the town of Kifl. While marching on Kifl, the Manchester Regiment was surprised in its camp and almost massacred. Major General Leslie lost 180 men with another 160 captured. There was near panic.

But the Cabinet in London was distracted by the guerrilla war in Ireland as well as by the counterrevolution in Russia. After all the glowing reports from Baghdad by Miss Bell and other "Arabists," there was disbelief that 130,000 locals were actually in arms against Britain. The crisis worsened in August as the uprising reached the upper Euphrates and the outskirts of Baghdad; outbreaks in the Kurdish north soon followed. Rebels cut off rail links to Persia and captured a number of key towns, including Baquba and Shahraban, killing every English official they could lay their hands on.

Churchill pressed the RAF to proceed with work on gas bombs ("especially mustard gas") but was finally forced to break the budget by calling in Indian reserves. The tide began to turn against the insurgents. The British Army set a barbaric precedent by using poison gas shells, while the RAF dropped bombs, and according to historian David Omissi, "machine-gunned women and children as they fled from their homes." The slaughter was indiscriminate and coincided with the hanging of political prisoners in Baghdad.

In September T. E. Lawrence wrote a letter to the Sunday *Times* protesting the savagery of Britain's "friendly occupation gone wrong." It might well be republished in the *New York Times* today.

> Our government is worse than the old Turkish system. They kept 14,000 local conscripts embodied, and killed a yearly average of 200 Arabs in maintaining peace. We keep 90,000 men, with aeroplanes, armoured cars, gunboats, and armoured trains. We have killed about 10,000 Arabs in this rising this summer. . . . How long will we permit millions of pounds, thousands of Imperial troops, and tens of thousands of Arabs to be sacrificed on behalf of a colonial administration which can benefit nobody but its administrators?

3. THE DEVIL'S LABORATORY

Thanks to bombers, poison gas, and armored cars, the British finally regained control of the country in September 1920. Tough Indian Office types enforced a Carthaginian peace. Through Christmas, expeditions ranged across the rebel zones burning villages, executing suspects, confiscating livestock, and enforcing punitive fines.

Churchill, soon to be promoted to Colonial Secretary, continued to advocate aerial terror as the cheapest and most effective way of ruling "ungrateful volcanoes" like Iraq and other Muslim colonies. In March 1921 the RAF put the finishing touches to an "air control" plan that envisioned eight squadrons of aircraft (including two of bombers) plus six RAF armored car companies taking the place of most of the regular Army divisions.

The essence of the strategy, explained Wing Commander Chamier, was that retaliation should never be halfhearted. The RAF must inspire absolute terror. "All available aircraft must be collected; the attack with bombs and machine guns must be relentless and unremitting and carried on continuously by day and night, on houses, inhabitants, crops and cattle."

Miss Bell herself, along with Arab notables, attended a thrilling RAF demonstration of the new incendiary weapons it proposed to use on delinquent villages and recalcitrant tribes.

> It was even more remarkable than the one we saw last at the Air Force show because it was more real. They had made an imaginary village about a quarter of a mile from where we sat on the Kiala dyke and the two first bombs dropped from three thousand feet went straight into the middle of it and set it alight. It was wonderful and horrible. Then they dropped bombs all round it, as if to catch the fugitives, and finally fire bombs which even in the brightest sunlight made flares of bright flame in the desert. They burn through metal, and water won't extinguish them. At the end the armoured cars went out to round up the fugitives with machine guns.

Fiery death from the air, moreover, became punishment not only for armed rebellion, but even more commonly, for failure to pay taxes. As one of Churchill's biographers gently put it, in early June 1921 an "aerial action had been taken on the Lower Euphrates, not to suppress a riot, but to pressure certain villages to pay their taxes." When Churchill queried the appropriateness of using bombers to collect taxes, Sir Percy Cox replied that he was merely implementing the Churchill doctrine and rhetorically asked if the Secretary for War and Air really wanted "to stifle the growing infant" of airpower. Churchill immediately avowed, "I am a great believer in airpower and will help it forward in every way."

Bombing and strafing, as a result, became fiscal and administrative, as well as military, policy. Iraq, so to speak, became the devil's laboratory for the Colonial Office's new experiment in using airpower to control colonial populations. As Jonathan Glancey reminded readers of *The Guardian* last April: "Terror bombing, night bombing, heavy bombers, delayed action bombs (particularly lethal against children) were all developed during raids on mud, stone and reed villages during Britain's League of Nation's mandate."

From his new and higher perch in the Colonial Office in late 1921, Churchill observed with satisfaction that "aeroplanes are now really feared." He continued to lobby for use of poison gas in Iraq and elsewhere. When a Colonel Meinertzhagen, familiar with the horror of gas attacks on the Western Front, challenged the application of this "barbarous method of warfare" to Arab civilian populations, he was harshly rebuked by Churchill, who replied, "I am ready to authorize the construction of such bombs at once."

Air control remained official policy through the 1920s, under Labour as well as Tory governments. One of the worst atrocities occurred in the late autumn and winter of 1923–24, when the Bani Huchaim tribal group in the Samawa area of Iraq was unable to pay its taxes. On the verge of starvation amidst a severe water shortage, the Bani Huchaim pleaded destitution. As one historian emphasizes, "There was no suggestion that there had been any serious unruliness or disorder in the area." Nonetheless, they were given a forty-eight-hour ultimatum and then were set upon with bombers. The RAF officially recorded the slaughter of 144 people, including women and children.

Although occasional opponents at home, like George Landsbury, denounced "this Hunnish and barbarous method of warfare against unarmed people," it was the foundation of the puppet throne upon which the British employed the foreign Hashemite prince, Faisal, in 1921. His election, by 96 percent of his new subjects— the triumph of Miss Bell's "Arabist" cause—was a rigged plebiscite orchestrated by the corrupt sheiks and notables and patrolled by the RAF. The real winner was the Iraq Petroleum Company and its London shareholders.

As one world-weary veteran of empire would observe in 1925: "If the writ of King Faisal runs effectively throughout his kingdom it is entirely due to British aeroplanes. If the aeroplanes were removed tomorrow, the whole structure would inevitably fall to pieces."

This history, probably unknown to most members of Congress—Democrat as well as Republican—who endorsed the U.S. attack on Iraq, remains, of course, a poisonous memory to all Iraqis. More broadly, ordinary people in the Muslim world recall that they were the original guinea pigs upon whom the European colonial powers, starting in Libya in 1911–12, perfected the terror bombing of civilian populations. The road to Guernica, Warsaw, Dresden, and Hiroshima began on the banks of the Euphrates and the flanks of the Atlas. In addition to Iraq, the RAF inflicted the "Churchill Doctrine" on civilian Egyptians, Palestinians, Somalis, Sudanese, Yemenis (Aden), and Afghanis in the 1920s. In the same decade, the Spanish and the French bombed and gassed the rebel villages of the Morrocan Rif. Who were the "terrorists" then?

REGARDING HOW TO GO ABOUT COMBATING BOMBER JETS,
GUIDED MISSILES, AND OTHER ULTRAMODERN TECHNOLOGICAL
INSTRUMENTS OF MASS DESTRUCTION

*This text was written just a few days before the "Coalition" bombing and the
subsequent colonizing campaign (or maybe it is more correct to say "privatizing
campaign") began. Rereading the text I wrote then, I cannot overcome the sadness
that comes from knowing that a certain reality has been stolen. The U.S. did invade
and now controls Iraq and its natural resources. The U.S. is trying by all means to
divide the Iraqi population by ethnic and religious factions in order to better domi-
nate them. Nonetheless, something tells me that the Muslim teacher is still teaching
with the same dedication as always; the boy with the enormous ears still yawns in
the morning; the man who sells dried fruit still opens his stand . . . but who knows,
any one of them could be one of the more than 10,000 "collateral damage" Iraqi
lives that this war has claimed. The only thing that I know for certain—which is
confirmed by the news that I hear every day about the resistance—is that the war
machine is, and forever will be, incapable of stealing from people and nations their
most powerful weapons: hopes and dreams. Let this text testify to that conviction.*

MARCH, 2003
While walking the streets of Baghdad, one tends to forget that one is in a city
on the brink of war. Here children scurry in the dust, men attend to their business,
young women dressed in tight velvet skirts laugh, talk, and flirt, their hair covered
with shawls that give them the seductiveness of mystery. The faces of Iraqi women
still must be counted among the most beautiful in the world.

One cannot help thinking that danger should be most tangible in the neighborhoods and along the avenues of a city over which looms the menacing presence of
hundreds of thousands of soldiers and Marines armed with the most sophisticated
killing equipment ever created. One might think that panic would be widespread and
constant in the face of a seemingly imminent "conventional" bombardment that may
have results not so different from those of the not-so-conventional bombs that fell on
Hiroshima and Nagasaki. One might think such things, but one would be mistaken.
In Baghdad, life continues as if there were no evident danger. University students
arrive on time for their Spanish-language classes, and as they talk with us, the Spanish
and Latin-American human shields, they seem more surprised by the idea that there
are Muslims on the other side of the world than by the possibility that in a few days
Baghdad may be demolished, as it was in the times of the Mongolian invasions.
Teenagers play soccer in the cluttered alleys that characterize the poor neighborhoods
of this river city. Shias celebrate the Day of the Massacre in the same way they have
done since the first time the Umma was divided with blood, less than a century after
the death of the Prophet[1] (s.a.w.s).[2]

It's not that people have no concept of the magnitude of the threat, but rather, under the deterministic view that characterizes the Islamic vision of life, *"insallah"* (if God wishes) is the key phrase. *Insallah* we will defeat the Americans. *Insallah* we will live, and of course, *insallah* we will die.

Because of this, it seems, the people most worried by the consequences of a bombardment are not those city inhabitants over whom hovers the sword, but rather the hundreds of foreigners, coming from all the trenches of the planet, who daily connect to the Internet and read the online versions of the *New York Times, The Guardian, El País,* and even *La Jornada* with something similar to the morbid feeling of someone who attends a horror movie in order to experience the adrenaline rush created by fear. For them, every announcement of war seems a villain more terrible than Jason from *Friday the 13th,* and each glimpse of peace a benevolent hero coming to the rescue. The locals, however, are not so misled. Perhaps *insallah* is in reality the only certainty that we can grasp: *insallah* that the gathering of the Horsemen of the Apocalypse in the Azores (Bush, Blair, and Aznar) is not the first trumpet; *insallah* that the United Nations will end its criminal embargo and that children in the Saddam Hussein Pediatric Hospital will get antibiotics and other basic medicines; *insallah* that the highly educated archeologist-turned-tour-guide with whom I met in Babylon will be able to return to his excavations and also fulfill his dream of visiting our Mayan ruins. *Insallah, insallah, insallah.*

Day to day, big and small *insallahs* come to pass: Allah grants us life for another day. A man waters the plants in front of his house. A Sunni teacher hurries to get to the El-Iptijar junior high school where she teaches girls, Sunnis as well as Christian and Shia students. A sleepy boy with a pair of enormous ears rubs his eyes and yawns as he boards the bus that will take him to grade school.

And this is the way to fight against bomber jets, guided missiles, and other ultramodern technological instruments of mass destruction: Living through every day, loving, studying, working, uprooting the nightmare of invasion from our sleep. As we were told by the man in charge at one of the many grain and dried fruit supply centers that exist in this town: If the Americans bomb, he still plans to open his business at the regular time, from ten in the morning to twelve at night, because what Bush wants is to paralyze the Iraqi people, terrorize them, and in the face of a people who bow only to *taqwa* (awe of God), a successful invasion may be a very hard thing to accomplish. *Insallah.*

1. The Day of the Massacre is the day in which al-Husayn, descendent of Muhammad (s.a.w.s.), was killed over differences about who was the rightful successor as Khalif. From this quarrel emerged the Shiites, who represent a large part of the Iraqi Muslim population.

2. The abbreviation "s.a.w.s." stands for "Salialahu alehi wa salaam," which means "May peace be upon him." As a Muslim, when I mention the name of the Prophet (s.a.w.s.), I say, write, or at least, think "Salialahu alehi wa salaam," for he brought salvation to humankind and we thank him thus.

United States Ambassador Paul Bremer during a meeting in his office in the Republican Palace.
LYNSEY ADDARIO/CORBIS 2003

BOMB BEFORE YOU BUY:
THE ECONOMICS OF WAR

This text is adapted from a speech delivered at McGill University in Montreal on October 25, 2003.

A couple of days after September 11, the *National Post* newspaper ran a story with the headline "Globalization Is So Yesterday." No one was interested in talking about the ravages of capitalism, we were told. The world was now focused on an entirely new set of issues: war, terror, and the clash of civilizations. Everything we thought we knew before September 11 no longer applied.

It was nonsense, of course. But it is true that many of us in the globalization movement were caught somewhat flat-footed by the military upsurge of these last two years. Yes, many of us instinctively made the transition from trade issues to antiwar activism, but we were not able, at first, to fully connect how warfare is used to enforce the very economic policies we had been fighting against.

The antiwar movement, for its part, faced a similar problem making these connections. The mainstream of the antiwar movement in North America focused almost exclusively on the visible atrocities of war: the violence, the human rights abuses, the broken international laws. When explaining *why* these wars were erupting, rarely did we surpass pat answers like, "It's about the oil." Some even argued that analyzing the economic model that sees war and occupation as market opportunities was "too divisive." Activists were urged to stay on message, to focus on the effects of war rather than its underlying causes.

I believe that this failure to marry the economic analysis of the globalization movement with the moral outcry of antiwar activism ended up hurting both movements. By failing to see the lengths to which capital will go to crack open new markets, the globalization movement seemed soft and naive. So did the antiwar movement: attempting to stop a war without directly confronting the economic system behind it is like trying to stop a bomb after it has already been dropped. In this context, peace never had a chance.

Fortunately, these artificial divisions are beginning to break down, because now that the war in Iraq is "over," the economic project behind the attack has emerged fully formed.

What is that economic program? It's the familiar one we in the globalization movement have been fighting against, enforced by the North American Free Trade Agreement (NAFTA), the World Trade Organization (WTO), the International Monetary Fund (IMF), the World Bank. It's a model that is sometimes called "globalization" but which the Latin Americans call "neoliberalism" and the French call "Savage Capitalism." For my purposes here, I am going to call it "McGovernment," because it is a kind of economic franchise, a globally enforced set of policies designed to make the world safe for multinational corporations.

McGovernment has three key components:

- Mass downsizing of the public sector. This makes sure that investors enjoy low taxes and low wages from a "flexible" workforce. It also starves the public sector, making it seem useless and inefficient and thus primed for . . .
- Mass privatizations. Privatizations give multinationals infinite investment opportunities to buy up public services and natural resources.
- Mass deregulation. This falls into two categories: The first form of deregulation is designed to eliminate the supports that protect local businesses, such as subsidies and restrictions on foreign ownership, thus eliminating the local competition for multinationals. The second form of deregulation is designed to remove all restrictions on the mobility of foreign capital, such as rules that require companies to keep some of their profits in the country where they made them.

So there you have it: the universal recipe for McGovernment—downsize, privatize, and deregulate. The result of all this corporate lubrication can be seen around the world in the commodification of ever more parts of the public sphere, from schools and hospitals to seeds and water.

In rich countries like ours, these economic policies are introduced relatively gradually. In poor countries they are introduced quickly, enforced by the International Monetary Fund in exchange for loans. When these policies were introduced in Argentina in the 1990s, the transformation of society was so rapid and so devastating that President Carlos Menem called the reforms "surgery without anesthetic." In Chile, when the reforms were introduced under Pinochet, they were called "shock treatment." In Russia, the IMF called it "shock therapy."

What is going on in Iraq right now makes those reforms look like spa treatments. Radical economic reforms that are usually spread out over decades are being rammed through in six months. Iraq's shock therapy has been implemented through "shock and awe" military force.

Iraq, as we all know, is a rich country. It has an embarrassment of natural resources and public services that have yet to be privatized; this is true for much of the Arab world. Oil wealth has kept Arab countries relatively outside the world trade system. Even in U.S. ally nations like Saudi Arabia and Kuwait, the oil companies, along with much else, are still owned by the government.

The growth represented by these untapped markets has become irresistibly tantalizing. Why? Because capitalism functions like a drug addict, and its drug of choice is growth; without a fix, it dies. And fixes are hard to come by these days. It's not just that the stock market hasn't recovered since its pre-9/11 bust. It's also that some of the market's most reliable suppliers of the growth drug have, of late, been holding out.

From the U.S. and European perspective, it used to be that if there was one thing you could count on in matters of international trade, it was the desperation of the poor. No matter how bad the deal, it was always better than nothing. But all of a sudden, poor countries are banding together and busting up trade rounds, standing up to the International Monetary Fund, and even turning down foreign investment.

Across Latin America, privatizations are being stopped in their tracks; oil pipelines are being resisted by local populations from Nigeria to Colombia; gold and copper mines are being rejected because their ecological cost is greater than their economic benefits. Center-left candidates have come to power in Brazil and Ecuador, promising to govern in the interest of the poor. In Argentina, popular protests pushed out the neoliberal government of Fernando de la Rua. Meanwhile, Hugo Chavez has held on in Venezuela despite the most dogged attempts by the elites in that country and in the U.S. to throw him out. And just last week in Bolivia, massive political protests forced president Gonzalo Sanchez de Lozada to resign. The uprising was sparked by an unpopular plan to sell the country's natural gas to the United States. The Free Trade Area of the Americas (FTAA) is hugely unpopular across Latin America, and the World Trade Organization talks just collapsed in Cancún. Poor countries are saying, we have tried these policies and they made us poorer, hollowed out our collective wealth—we don't want more of the same.

Free Trade Lite, which wrestles market access through backroom bullying during trade negotiations, isn't working anymore. That's why the market is getting desperate. That's why the Bush crew has stopped asking and started grabbing, upgrading Free Trade Lite to Free Trade Reloaded, which seizes new markets on the battlefields of war.

And that is precisely what the Iraq attack has been about. Bush has openly said that he wants a Free Trade Zone in the Middle East within a decade. It's the next project after the creation of the FTAA, and it all starts with Iraq. Iraq is the foothold, the wedge into an entire region that represents a massive new market opportunity. Senator John McCain put it well: Iraq, he said, is "a huge pot of honey that's attracting a lot of flies."

The "honey" isn't just the oil. It's also the water, the phones, the roads, the schools, the media, the trains, the planes, the jails, and anything else that can be turned into a commodity and sold for profit. The flies are named Bechtel, Halliburton, MCI, ExxonMobil, Wackenhut, TimeWarner, Wal-Mart, Boeing, NewsCorp, DynCorp, and on and on.

But before I go any further, let's make one thing absolutely clear: the United States government must compensate the Iraqi people so they can rebuild their country. The U.S. owes Iraq huge war reparations; it is a moral duty and it must be met. The problem is that the vast majority of the money for Iraq isn't going to the Iraqi people for reparations, for them to spend however they decide. It is being parceled out to U.S. firms selected by the Bush administration, for something called "reconstruction."

When you hear the word "reconstruction," it sounds perfectly benign. What could be wrong with Americans going to Iraq to rebuild bombed-out bridges and hospitals? It sounds like the Peace Corps. Only these companies aren't going to Iraq just to rebuild it—they are going there to buy it. As we speak, the country is being transformed into a giant shopping mall for U.S. (and a few British) multinationals.

It's the sale of the century: "Bomb Before You Buy."

Immediately after the war began, we started hearing about huge reconstruction contracts being handed out by the United States Agency for International Development (USAID). They were handed out in secret, without open bidding, to a handful of U.S. firms. And there was something new going on: Contracts to rebuild schools and hospitals which used to go to UNICEF or the Red Cross (nonprofit humanitarian agencies) were going to private education and health care corporations, companies that push privatization in the U.S. and Canada and see schools and hospitals as market opportunities.

And then there's Bechtel. Bechtel has a contract now worth more than $1 billion to oversee the rebuilding of roads, bridges, the electricity grid, and more. Many Iraqi entrepreneurs are angry that these jobs, which could help them get their economy running again, are going to Americans. The answer from Washington: Iraqi reconstruction is our booty—we bombed it, we bought it.

Anger at Bechtel is also mounting in Iraq because they aren't doing a very good job. According to a recent article in *The Economist*, in five months Bechtel has managed to rebuild a one-mile road bypass. Of the forty-nine bridges damaged during the attack, rebuilding work has only begun on three. Half of Baghdad's phone lines are still out.

And of course we have to talk about Halliburton, where Vice President Dick Cheney used to work as CEO. Cheney still retains Halliburton stock options and has been paid more than $350,000 in deferred compensation since taking office, but he nevertheless accuses anyone who calls that a conflict of interest of taking "cheap shots."

Allow me to be cheap: Halliburton has so far been paid $1.4 billion for its work in Iraq (its contracts can go as high as $7 billion). What is important to understand is how badly Halliburton needed this cash injection. Last year the company looked as if it was about to go the way of Enron. It was mired in accounting scandals and lawsuits; indeed, Halliburton posted a $500 million loss last year. One of its subsidiaries, Kellogg Brown and Root, was on the verge of filing for bankruptcy. Now Halliburton's share price is up 77 percent—not bad for a market slump—and it posted a $26 million profit last quarter.

The bottom line is that, as CEO, Dick Cheney got Halliburton into all kinds of trouble, but as Vice President, he saved Halliburton's butt—that's no exaggeration.

So what is Halliburton doing for the money? It is playing two key roles, and both of them have to do with privatization. The first is protecting Iraq's oil supply—putting out oil fires and repairing pipelines—so it can eventually be privatized. The second involves the rapid privatization of the U.S. Army. George W. Bush has decided that the Army's "core competency" is combat and that everything outside out that can be farmed out to temps. Halliburton has become the U.S. military's temp agency. Its temp soldiers build the army bases, cook the food, clean the latrines, do the soldiers' laundry, and cut their hair, all at cheaper salaries, of course, with the profits going back to Halliburton. One-third of the Iraqi mission is subcontracted to private companies.

So let's recap. The U.S. government, looking for new investment opportunities for its ailing firms, waged an unprovoked war with a partially privatized army, cleaning up afterwards using many of the same for-profit companies. But here's the kicker: When everything is cleaned up, America is going to sell Iraq off in pieces to these very same companies. I wish I could say that it was going to sell Iraq off to the highest bidder, but it's actually selling the embattled country off to the highest Bush-Cheney campaign donor.

The reconstruction of Iraq has already begun to seamlessly segue into the privatization of Iraq.

The real goal is now clear: The U.S government aims not just to rebuild Iraq's roads, but to turn them into privately owned and operated highways. It aims to not simply reconstruct the bombed-out water system, but to sell it to a company that will charge highly profitable rates for access. It aims to not just put out the oil fires and fix the oil pipelines, but to sell them entirely.

Bush, Donald Rumsfeld, and Paul Bremer now openly admit that they envision the "reconstruction" of Iraq as a remaking of it into a deregulated free-market economy. As journalist Robert Fisk pointed out, Bremer's choice of clothing says it all: a business suit with combat boots. In August Bremer wrote a memo containing policy instructions to the Iraqi Council—a body he hand-picked—in which he complained that Iraq's economy was too "protectionist" and dominated by "socialist economic dogma." He stated that Iraq must "pry open" most of its "industries for foreign investment." Sure enough, on September 19, 2003, two hundred Iraqi state firms were put up for privatization. Reconstruction has turned into the auctioning off of an entire country—someone else's country.

And according to new laws introduced by Bremer, U.S. firms can retain 100 percent ownership of banks, mines, and factories of all kinds. The only exception is oil, but this too will come. And who is going to buy all these Iraqi companies? The same U.S. firms that took part in the reconstruction.

Let's look at Bechtel again. On the global stage, Bechtel is one of the most aggressive proponents of the privatization agenda; one of its primary businesses is convincing foreign governments to sell off their water systems. Indeed, Bechtel was thrown out of Bolivia because, after it privatized the water in Chochabamba, prices escalated by 50 percent. Bechtel even deemed it illegal to collect rainwater (which it claimed was unfair competition). But in Iraq, Bechtel doesn't have to convince foreign governments to sell them the water, because there is no foreign government, just the U.S. government selling to U.S. corporations in foreign countries.

It's quite an amazing feat: they have actually managed to cut out the middleman.

What is going on in Iraq has never been about reconstruction—it has always been about privatization disguised as reconstruction, mass robbery masquerading as reparations.

A new company called New Bridge Strategies has been launched by Joe Albaugh, Bush's former campaign manager. It specializes in helping U.S. companies take advantage of Iraq's "unprecedented opportunities." One of the company's partners described the opportunities this way: "Getting the rights to distribute Procter and Gamble products can be a gold mine. One well-stocked 7-Eleven could knock out thirty Iraqi stores; a Wal-Mart could take over the country." There it is, the economic project behind this war: a massive new market, bombed into being.

But before Iraq can be turned into a free-market Mecca, a few more things have to happen. I talked earlier about McGovernment, but McGovernment isn't just about privatization; it also has to be about downsizing and deregulation.

Rest assured that Bremer is moving full steam ahead on both those fronts. Regarding downsizing, in his first month in Iraq Bremer fired more than 400,000 Iraqis without pensions or re-employment programs. He called these mass layoffs of state employees "de-Baathification"—the purging of Saddam Hussein's party officials from government. Of course, some of that was necessary in order to clean out Saddam Hussein's henchmen and propagandists, but Bremer's layoffs went much further. Low-level civil servants with no ties to the party have been fired en masse. In the name of "de-Baathification" he launched a full-scale attack on the public sector. Why? For the same reason the public sector is attacked here at home: to create opportunities for privatization, to create a flexible workforce willing to work for less, and to lower the tax burden.

So with privatization and downsizing taken care of, what's needed to finish the McGovernment package is deregulation. When Bremer and Bush talk about bringing "the free market to Iraq," it sounds like Iraqi businesses are going to have all sorts of wonderful new opportunities. Yet we know that hasn't been the case during reconstruction (now jokingly referred to in Iraq as "the full-Halliburton employment program").

But there are other ways that Iraqi businesses are being pushed out. When Bremer arrived, Iraqi-owned companies were obviously in rough shape; they had been pummeled by almost thirteen years of sanctions and two months of looting,

United States troops from the 101st Airborne Division work out of the battle command center of the Division Main Headquarters in one of Saddam Hussein's former palaces. LYNSEY ADDARIO/CORBIS 2003

not to mention two wars. So it would have made sense—if the U.S. were serious about rebuilding Iraq's economy—to concentrate on getting the electricity and phones operational, as well as providing the parts and materials needed for Iraq's damaged factories. But that's not what Paul Bremer did. Instead, just twenty-six days after the war was declared "over," with the lights and phones still off in Baghdad, Bremer flung open Iraq's borders to foreign multinationals; overnight, the market was flooded with cheap TVs, food, and clothes. What happened next was entirely predictable—hundreds of Iraqi companies were wiped out.

Once again, Iraq isn't being rebuilt; it is being erased. First by war, then sanctions, then war again, then looting, and now by absurdly unfair foreign competition which never gave Iraq's industries a chance to survive. Why? Well, the erasure of Iraqi firms is good news for foreign multinationals wanting a piece of Iraq's action; it's easier to get your Wal-Mart or 7-Eleven if the local competition has already been helpfully decimated.

Bremer has given these foreign investors other goodies too. On the same day that he put those two hundred state companies up for sale, he also announced that foreign firms doing business in Iraq would get tax breaks—from 15 to 45 percent—even more generous than those Bush has been handing out at home. He also removed all restrictions on taking profits out of the country.

From a foreign investor's perspective, Iraq is a dream come true. Everything that these companies lobby for at home but never receive in their entirety—because of this pesky thing called democracy—has been generously handed to them in Iraq. The country is a blank slate on which the most ideological Washington neoconservatives are designing their dream economy: fully privatized, downsized, deregulated, and open for business. Donald Rumsfeld said recently that "Iraq will have some of the most enlightened and inviting tax and investment laws in the free world."

But there's just one catch, and it's a big one: Iraq isn't part of the free world, because it isn't free.

In fact, it's under occupation, which means that the decisions about Iraqi society's core nature—how much foreign ownership of its economy will be allowed, whether it will have a public or private health-care system, how it will make use of its oil revenues—are being made without the consent of its people. Why? Because once the Iraqis have their own government, they might decide that they don't want to sell their country to Bechtel and Halliburton. But once the contracts are signed, it's all over. If the Iraqi people, once they have democracy, decide they want to change course, it will mean breaking signed contracts, expropriating assets, changing the terms of agreements, and the U.S. will not stand for that.

In the name of democracy, the Iraqi people are being robbed of the most basic democratic principle: the right of sovereign people to govern themselves and decide their collective destiny. Just as Iraq entered the so-called free market in the dark, they will now enter democracy handcuffed to key economic decisions already made for them. Then they will be told to hurry up and vote for their new leaders, just in time for Bush's reelection campaign.

As we all know, it's too late to stop the war. But if we act now, there is just enough time to deprive Iraq's invaders of the myriad economic prizes that are the *reason* they went to war in the first place. And this is the task faced by both the globalization and the antiwar movements: to try to stop the economic looting of Iraq.

BAGHDAD JOURNAL #2

Our first stop is the Iraq Assistance Center, where we found the public affairs office and picked up our free cell phones from MCI, courtesy of the U.S. taxpayers. It was Friday afternoon, the Muslim Sabbath; Baghdad felt like a ghost town. Beyond the ruined buildings, garbage was heaped in the streets, razor wire everywhere. The sense that we journeyed through an abandoned city increased when we reached the compound. Tumbleweeds drifted across the dirty street and caught on the razor wire.

The Iraq Assistance Center was originally a convention center used primarily by those close to Saddam, and most Baghdad residents had never been inside it. Now it sits surrounded by three sets of barriers and is guarded by tanks and GIs wilting in the heat. After five sets of checkpoints, we got inside, leaving behind us at the gate Iraqi men and women pleading for answers about missing sons and husbands. We weren't Iraqi and did not need assistance, so we could enter.

Inside the compound it was nearly deserted; we were told by the woman at the MCI trailer it was because of the Fourth of July. Later I remembered it was also Friday, always a quiet day in Iraq. After a stop in the lovely air-conditioned trailer provided by MCI which serves as a communication center, we passed through the security checkpoint—this time there was a body search, so a woman GI was called inside to attend us. We entered into the great hall and climbed the grand staircase to the second floor, where we were greeted by friendly reservist Mark Ingram from Oklahoma, a sixties holdout who laughingly complained that his toe rings were digging the daylights out of him. He joked as he handed us a form that "you too can play army and be embedded with a unit," adding that it was safer to do so during the invasion. Like most of the soldiers we spoke to, he wanted a real bed and three hot meals instead of a hard, wooden, bug-infested cot and barely edible Meals, Ready-to-Eat (MREs). All of the Bush administration's talk of "supporting the troops" is exposed as empty rhetoric when you see how these soldiers are actually living, overstretched and undersupplied in an attempt to prove that America can fight a war on the cheap. When we had left the states, the administration was planning to cut the troops' hazard pay, even though more U.S. soldiers are being killed and injured per day than during the period of "major combat" that Bush proclaimed over on May 1.

One of our objectives was to meet with Margaret Bhadi, Paul Bremer's advisor on gender affairs, to apply whatever pressure we could on the Coalition Provisional Authority (CPSA) to include a representative number of women on the Iraqi Governing Council that would supposedly serve as a transitional parliament on Iraq's road to democracy. To arrange the meeting we needed to go to the palace where the CPA had its headquarters. Sergeant Ingram pointed us to the shuttle bus that ran to the palace.

You meet the most interesting people waiting for that shuttle: CPA employees looking as if they'd just stepped off a golf course; GIs; businessmen; evangelists from Florida and Georgia here to bring humanitarian aid and the salvation of Jesus. The majority of Americans we met were from the South, including most of the GIs and the CPA employees. I strike up a conversation with one of them, who tells me he is "running operations" in Baghdad. He is a friendly fellow, a bit flirtatious, so I play along: "Will you take me on a tour of Baghdad?"

Sure, he says, now that they've gotten everything "back to normalcy" here.

"Normalcy—what does that mean to you?" I ask.

"You should have been here a few weeks ago," he says to me with a smile. "We have things running now."

I ask him if he's making fun of me. I tell him that I've just arrived to a sort of hell outside these walls and that this is far from normal. I was here in February, I tell him, and this is not what "normal" looks like. The playfulness ends and he goes back to talking to the men gathered with him.

I press on, ask him his qualifications for this job. "I was on the Atlanta police force for thirty years and have taken classes in management," he responds.

Again I think he's pulling my leg, but as I continue to question him, I realize that he's serious. I ask if they see much of the city, and he tells me no: "It's not safe out there."

The rundown shuttle that takes us to the palace is driven by a Kellogg Brown and Root employee from Savannah, Georgia, who was a trucker back home, but the money is better here. Regardless, he tells me he can't wait to get back home.

"Why can't the Iraqis drive this bus?" I ask.

"No one trusts them," he replies. "The only jobs the Iraqis have at the Assistance Center are menial or as translators, but they might be let go," he informs me. "They've been seen pacing

through the compound, and the fear is that they might be giving target information to the 'terrorists' and 'remnants of Saddam's regime' who are attacking American targets." He is sweating and tired of the back and forth.

The palace is the exercise in excess that you would expect from contemporary accounts of Saddam's regime: it's dripping with gold and velvet, all ostentation and stupidity. Bremer's offices are arranged around a huge rotunda with marble walls, a gold dome, and stained-glass windows; it's protected by a security system like those at an airport, with green lights flashing up and down the side, flanked by green marble columns. We nickname his office "Oz." We can hardly believe that the CPA has chosen to make its home in this place, this symbol of oppression and corruption. I remember a quote from General Tommy Franks during the invasion about how we aren't bombing the palace because we will soon own it.

We notice a flyer on a partition by

United States Ambassador Paul Bremer walks through the Republican Palace after a meeting with the Ministry of Finance. LYNSEY ADDARIO/CORBIS 2003

Bremer's meeting room for a Fourth of July party. It promises fresh lobster tails and shrimp, a visit from the "Original Terminator," Arnold Schwarzenegger, and across the flyer is printed "Hasta

A U.S. soldier jumps off a high diving board at a Fourth of July celebration at one of Saddam Hussein's main palaces in Baghdad. LYNSEY ADDARIO/CORBIS 2003

La Vista, Baby"—"beer and barbeque at Saddam's pool at 5:00 pm."

It's just five o'clock, so we decide to find the party.

Outside we see GIs heading toward a line of palm trees. We pass a trailer and stop to ask a female GI for directions. "What's in the trailer?" we ask.

"The laundry," she responds. "The NGOs and higher-ups in the CPA drop off their dry cleaning here and it gets sent to Kuwait to be done."

I ask, given the 65 percent jobless rate in Iraq, whether it wouldn't make sense to do the laundry here.

The GI shrugs her shoulders and says, "Nothing makes sense to me these days," and points us to the entrance of the pool area.

We could hear the laughter, the splashing, and the music before we entered, but we were not prepared for what we saw.

The pool area, supposedly favored by Saddam's wife, looks like the back of an elegant hotel. It's landscaped with vast manicured lawns and rows of tall palms, and the centerpiece is an enormous tiled pool with a fountain in the middle with synchronized jets of water; there's also a huge high dive that holds up to ten people. As we entered, groups of GIs did cannon-balls together off the platform. Bagpipe music played over a PA system. Tables are decorated in red-white-and-blue bunting, barbeques grill hot dogs and burgers, and tubs are full of beer, but I do not see the promised lobster tails and shrimp.

Not many people were in the pool. I asked one female GI why she wasn't swimming. "Who thought to bring a swimsuit?" she replied. A few women ventured into the shallow water in sports tops and shorts. Everyone gathered together in sort of self-segregated clumps: white, black, gay, and occasionally men mingling with women, all having their first beers since their deployment.

Most of the people who are courageous enough to approach us are businessmen, most of whom are from the South. I look around, hoping to find a new story in the crowd, and I see someone who looks intellectual, slightly Southern Californian, has a ponytail, and keeps his distance from the crowd. I introduce myself and learn from him that before coming to Baghdad he had taught religion and political philosophy at a private, conservative college in Southern California. "I'm Bremer's intelligence advisor on the Shiites," he tells me. He talks about the reports he prepares for Bremer each day which determine how the CPA should respond to the Muhajedeen who are trying to find their place in the new power structure. I ask a question about fundamentalists, and he tells me the people here are extremists—everyone is a fundamentalist. I am shocked by his arrogance and his banter, which is Machiavellian at best. He misses Southern California, he tells me, and has sent home for his roller blades. "I'm only here for six months; I can take it. The work we do here is extremely important," he wants me to know.

"We're going to take a page from Saddam's book," he says with an insider's confidence. "Fear is the foundation of any government. If you make a dog hungry, he'll follow you anywhere."

I find myself too uncomfortable with what he is saying, so I ask for his number and where he is staying to try again with him later. The sun has started to set behind the palace. Bremer was to have addressed the party, but he's been delayed by some bad news: an audiotape purportedly by Saddam has surfaced. We get this information from a man who says that he is Bremer's valet and the organizer of this event. Currently he's fretting about securing a karaoke machine for tomorrow's entertainment. He invites us to join him for a tour of the sex toys and wild animals at Uday's palace. We decline. It's getting late, and we are in the middle of a compound with no clear way to get back to the Andaluz— and we've been warned to be inside by 8 P.M. The DJ starts to play the Rolling Stones: "You Can't Always Get What You Want." We notice the Iraqi men in blue sailor outfits circulating through the grounds, emptying the trash.

The valet gets on his walkie-talkie and arranges for a Humvee and two lieutenants to take us to the back gate, where we can get a taxi. We feel the fear as we stand on a Baghdad street at dusk and hail a cab.

Continued . . .

AMERICAN MUSLIMS AND IRAQ

> *. . . It's getting cold in California*
> *I guess I'll be leaving soon*
> *Daylight fading*
> *Come and waste another year*
> *All the anger and the eloquence are bleeding into fear . . .*
> —Counting Crows, "Daylight Fading," from *Recovering the Satellites* (1996)

I am a Canadian Muslim and also an academic who studies Islam. My doctoral dissertation was on Muslim communities in Toronto, and my own work is on Muslim communities in North America. Since 1997 I have been living in the United States while teaching in the Department of Religious Studies at California State University, Northridge. With the terrorist attacks on September 11, 2001, Islam and violence became synonymous in the minds of many people. More than twenty years earlier, the Iranian revolution (and its aftermath) first alerted many people in North America to the role of violence in the contemporary Muslim world. While many people consider Islam to be a religion of violence, many Muslims consider Islam to be a religion of peace. Clearly, anyone teaching courses in the study of Islam has to be aware that he or she cannot criticize, promote, or be objective about Islam and Muslims without taking a political stand.[1]

After the war on Afghanistan, when it became clear that Iraq would be the next target, a number of us did what we could to assert our opposition to that upcoming war. At my university the following letter (incorporating passages from a letter circulated by the Fellowship of Reconciliation) was drafted and signed by a large number of faculty and staff in the fall of 2002:

> We, the undersigned members of the academic community at California State University, Northridge, are opposed to an invasion of Iraq by the United States. We remember the words of the Reverend Dr. Martin Luther King Jr., who on April 4, 1967, during the Vietnam war said: "Some of us who have already begun to break the silence of the night have found that the calling to speak is often a vocation of agony, but we must speak. We must speak with all the humility that is appropriate to our limited vision, but we must speak."
>
> We are opposed to U.S. military aggression against Iraq. It is as simple as that. As educators, we do not want our children, grandchildren, or students to go to war. We have not been attacked by Iraq. We have, however, since the end of the Gulf War, punished the Iraqi people through a comprehensive program of sanctions. A million Iraqis have died in the past decade, and now we threaten them with war. Contrary to the rhetoric of President Bush, we do not live in fear, but we understand that much of the world lives in fear of us.
>
> International law, the United Nations charter, and the clear testimony

of most nations of the world all forbid invading another land to control its leadership, or to confront a hypothetical future threat.

Indeed, in the case of the Iraqi threat, it is all hypothetical. Last May, the U.S. State Department published a compilation of terrorist activity across the globe. There was no mention of Iraq in it and no evidence of Iraqi involvement in the awful September 11 attacks.

"No" is the word that must now be whispered in the soul, shouted from the rooftops, declared to our groups and contacts, proclaimed from our places of worship, taught in our schools, colleges, and universities, and find its way into the media even if many others would rather rush to conform.

We ask all persons of conscience to resist this unjust war. It will not be fought in our name. Now is the moment to say "NO."

At my university a peace and justice group was created in response to the impending war.[2] What was heartening to me as a Muslim was that I wasn't in any way the driving force behind this group. Our university has a large number of Central American students, a new Central American Studies program, and one of the oldest Chicano/a Studies programs in the country. Many of our students from countries like Nicaragua or El Salvador have experienced in their bodies the effects of American foreign policy. And for more than three decades our Chicano/a Studies faculty and students have spoken the truth to power.

When the war against Iraq inevitably came, the widespread opposition to the war came as a relief for Muslims in America. Many of us had worked tirelessly since the attacks on 9/11 to educate the public about Islam. We, as Muslims, were horrified by and condemned the attacks, and our sympathies and prayers were with the victims and not with the terrorists. In the year after the attacks, many of us grieved for this country—our country—and the loss of the very civil liberties that made it such a wonderful example for the rule of law.

The line that I have been repeating over and over to myself comes from a song by the local California band Counting Crows: "All the anger and the eloquence are bleeding into fear." We fear for our country—our home—and what will become of it. The Patriot Act erodes all of our freedoms, and its latest iteration promises to be much worse. More than 1,000 people are still detained without cause. Brave people, most notably Japanese Americans who have firsthand experience of where that particular road leads, have spoken out against the detentions. The artist Garry Trudeau has, with his usual brilliance, addressed the issue of the detainees in his Doonesbury comic strip.

We who are Muslim need your help. To borrow a line from the poet Langston Hughes, we too are America. There is so much that needs to be done for healing and reconciliation in this country. We praise God and rejoice in the number of people who are willing to do the hard work that lies ahead for all of us.

1. Tazim R. Kassam has written an excellent essay on the issues of teaching Islam post-9/11: "On Being a Scholar of Islam: Risks and Responsibilities," in *Progressive Muslims: On Justice, Gender, and Pluralism*, ed. Omid Safi (Oxford: Oneworld Publications, 2003), pp. 128–44.

2. The Web page for the group is http://www.csun.edu/~csunupj/.

Though United States officials, including United States President George W. Bush, declared the deaths of Saddam's sons definite, Iraqis still had doubts and demanded proof of their deaths. LYNSEY ADDARIO/CORBIS 2003

"WHATEVER YOU SELL CAN BE BOUGHT": AN INTERVIEW WITH KRISTINA BORJESSON

Kristina Borjesson, Emmy Award–winning journalist and editor of *Into the Buzzsaw: Leading Journalists Expose the Myth of a Free Press*, knows what it's like to be on either end of an intimidated news media. After a diligent investigation of the TWA Flight 800 tragedy led Borjesson to conclude that the doomed plane was downed by arms fire, the decorated journalist was summarily dismissed from CBS and nearly excommunicated from mainstream media altogether.

Such dangerous—sometimes deliberate—friction promises to obfuscate the picture of what is truly happening on the ground in Iraq for those turning to CBS, Fox, CNN, or other like-minded outlets. If anything, Borjesson would argue that conventional American media is the last place one should search for the truth about why we are in this quagmire, who is responsible, how it is ravaging lives on all sides, and what the future holds for Iraq's continually oppressed citizenry.

Sandra Fu: SF   *Kristina Borjesson:* KB

SF: *What do you think of the news media's handling of the Iraq situation?*

KB: I don't think the news media is handling it. First, let's go back to before the war and look at something very interesting. The mainstream media, whether it's radio, cable, or network TV, reaches a critical mass of people, and if information doesn't reach that critical mass, it basically doesn't exist. And most of the media's news sources were military people, Bush administration officials, and the pundits who agreed with them. Interestingly, at the same time Colin Powell was trying to sell the war to the UN using information that we now know was false, his son Michael Powell at the FCC was deciding whether or not the same media conglomerates that control the stations his father was using to sell the war could own more TV and radio outlets and establish an even larger presence in the market. What better time to sell a war when you have the mass media by the bottom line? Once we went to war, information was controlled through embedded journalists—there were very few voices emerging with real reportage. You didn't see the devastation, you didn't see thousands of civilians dead in the streets or their homes. And now in the postwar stage, we still really have no idea about what's going on, except from the soldiers, who are now apparently writing letters home to their parents, which in turn causes their parents to come forth and say, "Hey, our media isn't really telling us what's going on." Now citizens are doing the job for journalists! War is an extreme activity; billions of dollars are being spent to maintain this occupation, and for what purpose? Was it really to liberate the Iraqi people, which was the big selling point? Look at the current cabinet—the vice president, national security advisor, our secretary of state—these are people involved in the oil and arms industries. If you look at the chessboard and the pieces, it is very clear.

SF: *Did you notice a distinction between print media and broadcast media in the war/occupation coverage?*

KB: There was more analysis and in-depth coverage in print; this is always the case, for fundamental reasons. First of all, there's the nature of TV. As an audiovisual medium, TV conveys information more powerfully, but print is much better for providing detailed background information and analysis. There's been some good print coverage of the war and occupation, but compared to television reporting it didn't have much impact. Only TV has access to enough people at the same time to reach the mass public consciousness. Case in point: The *Christian Science Monitor* reported that right after 9/11, polling data showed that only 3 percent of Americans who were asked open-ended questions about who was behind the attacks mentioned Iraq or Hussein. But by January of this year [2003], 44 percent of Americans believed that "that either 'most' or 'some' of the September 11 hijackers were Iraqi citizens." This happened because "legitimate news sources," consisting primarily of Bush administration members, regularly went on TV and linked the Iraqis with 9/11. The fact that many reputable print outlets reported that Hussein wasn't connected to 9/11 didn't matter. There was a lot of good independent radio coverage on this too, but again, nothing hit the mass public consciousness; mainstream radio coverage basically mirrored mainstream TV.

Because TV is more powerful, the information it conveys about major events is more highly controlled. TV's primary purpose is marketing, not conveying information, so anything that's going to affect its marketing function—like reporting on controversial subjects, or reporting facts that aren't good for business or the administration in power—just won't happen. Mainstream print outlets are subject to marketing constraints too, but they still have more wiggle room than mainstream TV. Also, there are lots of independent print outlets as well as numerous Internet sites (which I consider print media, unless they have audiovisual components to them) which provide coverage that their bigger counterparts won't. Independent TV outlets providing coverage of major events like the war/occupation are practically nonexistent.

SF: *So many people seem to need to have the dots connected for them.*

KB: And the reason why is because the information given to them isn't coverage of anything specific. Tell us what's going on: Why can't somebody ask people who are directly involved? It's Reporting 101—if you have a problem, then you go to the people who have their hands on the problem. Mainstream media never does that.

SF: *Perception is reality, as advertisers say.*

KB: Exactly. Pundits come on the air and tell you what the American military has done that day, who got shot and where. They give you vignettes bereft of context.

SF: *Where should people turn for news that actually informs?*

KB: Foreign news sources, because they are more free to report on what the U.S. is doing than U.S. reporters are. People can go to the BBC. I happen to like *AsiaTimes* online; I think they do a great job of reporting in context. I think the Center for Public Integrity has a really good website. But people have got to make the effort. At this point, they actually have to seek good coverage, because they're not going to get it from network television. And it's annoying—why do you have to go to the Internet to get decent reporting? Shouldn't you be able to expect it from the networks? No, because there are conflicts between their business interests and the public service mandate.

SF: *Meanwhile, the truth about what's happening on the ground in Iraq gets lost along the way.*

KB: The truth rings true. You just have to go to firsthand news sources. If all of your journalists are nicely tucked away in tanks, then they're not going to be crossing to the other side where the missiles have fallen, where the bombs have exploded. They aren't going to record the devastation that America has caused, not so much to the opposing military, but to the people. America doesn't truly engage in hand-to-hand combat anymore; we're safe and comfortable while it is the civilians being killed instead of the opposing soldiers.

SF: *When CNN war correspondent Christiane Amanpour appeared on* Topic A With Tina Brown *on CNBC, she commented, "I think the press was muzzled, and I think the press self-muzzled. I'm sorry to say, but certainly television, and perhaps to a certain extent my station, was intimidated by the administration and its foot soldiers at Fox News. And it did, in fact, put a climate of fear and self-censorship, in my view, in terms of the kind of broadcast work we did." What do you think of Amanpour's statement, and what is the significance of it?*

KB: I salute Amanpour for speaking out. It is a very big deal that she did. I'm fascinated that she talked about the "administration and its foot soldiers at Fox News" creating a climate of fear at CNN. How, specifically, did they do that? She didn't really answer the question. She talked about questions not being asked and "disinformation . . . at the highest levels," but she didn't specifically address how the administration and Fox cowed reporters at CNN.

As CNN's crown jewel correspondent, Amanpour can get away with making a statement about the press muzzling itself, but don't expect a rash of journalists to follow with their views on slanted reporting and muzzling. Other journalists don't have the immunity from punishment that Amanpour enjoys by virtue of her star status. The others will come out when—if ever—it's safe to do so.

SF: *What does this mean for the American public?*

KB: The Amanpour interview? Speaking optimistically, it means another brick in the wall was taken out to give the American people a glimpse of what's really going on—actually, since we're talking about Amanpour, maybe two bricks. But there's still a lot of wall to tear down.

SF: *What about integrating the information coming from the countless Iraqi newspapers? Would that give us a more accurate view?*

KB: Absolutely, if news sources would do that. But the U.S. has a profound problem: we live as if we're the only nation on the planet. We don't care about what's going on in other countries. We don't care what happens to the populations that supply us with cheap shoes and shirts. We don't care who gets killed in Iraq—we want our cheap oil. America is extremely provincial; we know nothing about what our government or our businesses are doing in Iraq. We've lived with blinders on, and that's why 9/11 was such a shock. Saudi money was pumped into that tragedy, and yet they've suffered no consequences. But in Iraq, there's a dictator who, by the way, was our friend a few years ago.

SF: *People don't seem to care about that part.*

KB: When you say to them, "If you don't care about that, then how can you be horrified about 9/11?," then they say, "You're not patriotic." They don't seem to understand that we all have to live on this planet. It's full of countries, and we're in each and every one of them doing things that we wouldn't accept if any of them came here and tried the same. Look at Noriega—he was our man in Panama, yet when [George Herbert Walker] Bush needs to disassociate himself from the drug dealing he knew was occurring, what does he do? Turns Panama into a military operation and kills several thousand people. What if other countries came and did that here? Americans don't consider this; it's as if the people in those countries are less than human, as if their lives don't count. And if you don't care, that's fine, but be ready to pay the price. I'm from Haiti, and we have an expression there: "Pluck the chicken but don't make it scream." Well, the planet is America's chicken, we've been plucking it to death, and it's finally screaming at us. We're losing friends left, right, and center.

SF: *All of this seems to be a comment on the dangers of using just the government or military to supply you with crucial information.*

KB: Well, they can trust the mass media to put out what they say, no questions asked. Consider the poll that asked Americans if they believed Saddam Hussein was directly involved in 9/11. People answered yes, even though it was false. Why? Because that's what the administration was disseminating to the media and from there it sank into the national consciousness. This was a way for the administration to get to Iraq.

SF: *Fear is a tool of control.*

KB: The administration didn't care what the American people wanted; they disagreed with protesters and they disagreed with the UN. They used anything that suited their mission to sell this war, because anything they disseminated would be broadcast on national television—and in the case of Fox News—ardently defended. CNN used the same sources and floated what I call the "Bill Hemmer" or "Paula Zahn" questions, that is, nothing that would put the administration's feet to the fire. Whatever the administration had to throw at the people to get them to keep quiet, they did it. Think about it: If you're making money in arms and oil, you're going to make money on the war and the reconstruction. How much money have these people already made? How are the deals and accounts set up? Halliburton and Bechtel get no-bid contracts—how does that get kicked back? Why is Halliburton getting a no-bid clause? Who's working there? How is this working? Follow the money.

SF: *Meanwhile, the people in Iraq, especially the women, are being robbed of life's necessities.*

KB: Particularly outside of the United States, women are robbed of something as fundamental as an education. It's a huge issue, because what you have in many countries are societies where literally half the population has no viability beyond breeding. I'm wondering what would happen if there were real movements, real efforts to empower women, especially in those countries where it is culturally unacceptable. And when I say empower them, I mean educate them so they can become economically independent. It's hugely political, educating women, because then they have influence over the men they rear—that might make a difference. It's actually an avenue that's not explored enough, because not enough women care or pay attention.

SF: *Why do major media outlets ignore the women in these countries?*

KB: Women aren't the power centers. They have no power. In those countries, the crowds and leaders, almost always men, get the coverage.

SF: *It's alarming that women's issues aren't getting more coverage, given the fact that America cited women's hardships—in Afghanistan at least—as a chief reason why such countries need to be liberated in the first place.*

KB: You always have to keep this in mind: Whatever you sell can be bought, and if it turns out to be false, oh well. With Iraq, it was not just nuclear but also chemical weapons of mass destruction. It really doesn't matter if women aren't liberated once you actually get into Afghanistan, just as it won't eventually matter if weapons of mass destruction are found in Iraq. It's the Orwellian Ministry of Truth factor—the very opposite of what is true today could be reported tomorrow. Meanwhile, the other truth has disappeared, as if it didn't exist.

IRAQ, OR THE LAST PIECE OF THE MASK

I am a woman Islamist, an intellectual, and a citizen of the world. As a consequence, my reaction to the Iraqi tragedy—a tragedy occurring at a Dante-esque scale—is three-dimensional.

I am a woman, a human being naturally destined to give life and dispense love, not to wage war and partake in chaos. What's more, however, because I am an Arab-Muslim woman, what happens in Iraq and throughout the Third World only adds to the numerous and extremely painful bruises that my culture, and thus I, have experienced. It undermines my will to continue working to see this world, God willing, one day living in peace, *"as-salam."* This Arabic word, *"as-salam,"* not only means "peace," but it also refers to one of the names of God. And God chose this word for my Muslim brothers and sisters to use as a daily greeting: *"Assalamu alaykum,"* which means "May peace cover you."

From the mouth of a Muslim woman, such a greeting has not always been commonplace. In our society power has been usurped by cruel dictators like Saddam Hussein. As the outside world began to notice how Muslim women have experienced the repercussions of tyranny—in their societies, in their homes, and on their bodies—the assumption was made that Islam was and is our torturer. The perverted version of Islam that enslaves and oppresses Muslim women is not the Islam that God destined as a universal message of equity and spirituality. This false Islam is the sort that a man like Saddam Hussein adds to Iraqi nationalism in order to play on the emotions of the Muslim world.

Considering the sad state of affairs in Iraq, I would love to have been able to believe in the idea of the Good Samaritan country—be it the United States, England, or any other seemingly well-intentioned nation—coming to save us from the tyranny that the country had become mired in. My fellow sisters and I, who would have been the main beneficiaries of any truly liberating action from outside, looked forward to a meaningfully changed society where they could hope to find in men real and equal partners within the family structure or in the community as a whole. The fall of Saddam should have made me happy.

I would have loved to have believed the American propaganda, the promise of democracy and absolute Good defeating tyranny and absolute Evil. As one of many Islamic women struggling to regain my original rights granted by God, such a gift from Heaven would have pleased my soul.

I am saddened by the clear-eyed knowledge I now have that President Bush did not go to war for Good, or even against Evil, but for oil and in order to satisfy an appetite for domination which America no longer attempts to hide from the world. In the wake of the invasion and occupation, we are farther from democracy than ever before.

From my perspective as an Arab and Muslim woman and as a citizen of the world, the American system seems to serve primarily as a vehicle for the President to manipulate the people of the U.S. Cynicism has always been the hallmark of any

Realpolitik, but no power in the history of humanity has combined such will for domination with such a destructive arsenal as the United States today. While President Bush still makes a minimal effort to justify his actions in speeches and by superficial propriety, I fear that what has happened in Iraq will be the final unveiling of hypocrisy. When this happens, neither Americans nor any of the world's citizens will have the luxury of fooling themselves and ignoring the obvious any longer.

As a member of a movement that for thirty years has resisted the absurd policies of despotism with nonviolence, a glimmer of hope is seen each time we discover on the Internet, in a publication, or in a declaration, that other citizens of the world have as much desire as we do to bring common sense and humanity to government and society. It is good to know that there are truly virtuous people like Noam Chomsky, John Esposito, Scott Ritter, John Entelis, Richard Crane, José Bové, and hundreds of others who know how to say "no," who truly care about the ideas behind a global community. Their words and actions correspond perfectly to the spirit of Islam as referred to by Omar, valuable Companion of the Prophet, when he instructed his fellow citizens: "Do learn how to say 'no' [to injustice], loudly and with your whole being."

America has become the mirror of our absolute misfortune, but we must always remember that hope is the most basic necessity for political action, regardless of how tempting it is to react to irresponsible violence with irresponsible violence, to meet hatred with hatred. In the current situation it is our job as women, men, and Muslims to respond not through suicidal actions springing from unthinking anger, but rather in the most well-considered and socially aware manner possible.

Nahla Juwad waits for her sister outside of the Baquba Children's Hospital after an attack against American soldiers on the hospital grounds, mid-morning, July 26, 2003. LYNSEY ADDARIO/CORBIS 2003

A soldier with the 4th Infantry Division, 3rd Brigade, from the 1st Battalion–68th Armored Regiment, stands guard over detained Iraqis. LYNSEY ADDARIO/CORBIS 2003

THE CHANGING FACE OF OCCUPATION: WHAT NUMBERS CANNOT TELL

On April 10, 2003, the morning after Saddam's statue fell in one of Baghdad's central squares, an American soldier, chewing gum and blowing bubbles, sat atop his tank near the square and watched a young Iraqi man pushing a carriage full of medical equipment, computers, and an air-conditioner, all looted from the nearby al-Sadoon Hospital. Another soldier was standing on the roadside preventing people from approaching the square by holding up both hands and repeating "Go back, go back." There were no Iraqis in the square behind him, only American tanks and vehicles. This small scene tells a lot about the presence of the occupation forces in Iraq from the very beginning.

However, after six months of war and occupation, an essential change has occurred in the small scene described above. The soldier on the tank will no longer expose himself to danger in the streets; instead he has pulled back into hidden corners and surrounded himself with high sandbags and barbed wire. Baghdad's main streets are now filled with ugly barracks, checkpoints, and high walls at the entrance to public buildings, which block the traffic and create many problems. Entering these buildings now takes longer and is more difficult.

The other soldier will no longer use bare hands to prevent people from passing, nor will he shout in a monotone, "Go back." Instead he stands grim-faced, aiming his gun at passing Iraqis and using it unhesitatingly whenever someone fails to understand the message. Today there have been hundreds of casualties in mistaken, random, and indiscriminate shootings; many of them are women and children. The most flagrant was the killing of ten Iraqi policemen by American fire a week ago— this was the third time that U.S. soldiers killed a policemen.

Baghdad today is another city—everything has changed. The streets, buildings, and squares are almost deserted after 6 P.M., and they are devoid of women, whether at the money-changing tables lining the main streets, among the homeless children and families squatting in public buildings, with the camera-and-notebook-laden foreigners looking for the next story, or at the fuel queues snaking out of the petrol stations. However, the most significant change can be read on the Iraqi faces that articulate mounting bewilderment and shock.

The last six months in Baghdad have been too long—an age. For a nation that has been patient for decades and has undergone three wars, thirteen years of sanctions, political repression, and continual outside threats, six months has been too long to wait for relief, too long to wait for positive changes.

Given the casualties of war, the mass deaths inflicted by bombing, the chaos of looting, the immolation of public buildings, the shock of the rapid fall of the state, people now understand the real face of the occupation and its true meaning: negligence, lies, arrogance, and humiliation. In no time Iraqis have discovered that all the promises have led only to more empty promises projected into some unforeseeable future.

The problems of daily life, exacerbated by the existence of the occupying forces, lie heavily on the Iraqi people: insecurity; the absence of effective Iraqi authority; unemployment and accompanying fear of the future; constant shootings; stories of indiscriminate firing upon civilians; thousands of haphazard arrests for unknown reasons, with detainees taken to unknown places for undefined periods of time. These new conditions have been added to the existing realities of a deeply divided and impoverished Iraq.

In the midst of the current devastation, accurate statistics and numbers are illusive because the occupying forces deliberately attempt to conceal negative facts wherever possible, and significant events or trends are not systematically documented.

Iraq Body Count, a volunteer group of British and U.S. academics and researchers, has stated that 7,798 Iraqis were killed during the war (2,356 in Baghdad alone), and 20,000 were injured (8,000 in Baghdad). There are no statistics on the number of civilian casualties in Baghdad since May 1, 2003, the day President Bush declared the official end of the war, but Dr. Faiq, the director of Baghdad's forensic hospital, has said that based on bodies brought to the morgue, the average number of people killed daily is twenty to thirty. In July, for example, 720 people were killed, 470 of them shot. This is a 47 percent increase from July 2002. *Guardian* journalist Peter Beaumont, writing on September 14, 2003, put shooting-related deaths at 400 a month.

The occupying authorities, officially known as the Coalition Provisional Authority (CPA), bear the responsibility for this dramatic rise in murders, even if some of the killings were not by their forces. According to the 4th Geneva Convention, these authorities are fully responsible for the protection of the civilian population.

Although the first order of the occupying authorities was to provide for local authority, insecurity is the most important problem facing Iraqis. This insecurity has many causes, including the absence of real local authority; the inefficiency of the new Iraqi police, who lack weapons; the terrifying midnight raids mounted on Iraqis; and the occupier's negligence, withholding of logistical information and authority, unwillingness to jeopardize their soldiers' lives, and refusal to apply Iraqi law to the occupying countries' citizens.

Lately, many new kinds of crimes—killings in broad daylight, armed robberies, kidnappings, rapes, and car hijackings—have appeared. Mr. Abdul-Razaq Al-Ani, a judge at the New Baghdad court, says that in the space of two weeks there were 50 killings, 176 car thefts, 4 robberies accompanied by killings, and 2 kidnappings for ransom. The occupying authorities deal with the issue by focusing on the need for their soldiers' security. When Colin Powell was asked about security during a September 14 press conference in Baghdad, he spoke only of the personal security of U.S. soldiers. To him and other occupiers, security means eliminating armed resistance and nothing else.

Another pressing problem facing Iraqis is the occupation forces' power of arbitrary arrest. Often those arrested are unaware of exactly why they were arrested, and their families know neither where their loved ones are nor how long they will be held. According to Amnesty International, there are approximately thirty Iraqi prisons, with Baghdad Airport, Bucca in Basrah, and Tesfiraht the three largest prison camps. The official detainee population stands at 10,000, according to the occupation authorities, but the CPA lists do not necessarily represent all detainees, because these lists are updated infrequently and dozens of people are arrested daily. From former prisoners, stories of torture, bad treatment, and the denial of human rights are prevalent.

The country's devastated economic situation creates the ideal conditions for crime to flourish. The World Food Program report of June 6, 2003, stated that one-fifth of Iraqis suffer chronic poverty. The Iraqi Union of the Unemployed says there are currently ten million people (approximately 60 percent of the working-age population) unemployed in Iraq.

This year's war has added misery to the already suffering classes. In the Al-Thawra (now Al-Sadr) district of three million inhabitants—mostly farmers who immigrated to the capital over the last fifty years—four out of five families live in a house measuring, on average, two hundred square meters. Most of them are newly unemployed, widows, or disabled; the majority are ex–prisoners of war or soldiers released from service when the Iraqi army was dissolved after the war. Many families are homeless or squatting in deserted public buildings or schools. The schools in deprived areas are in inadequate buildings, basically large barracks without any furniture. There are 18 families (120 individuals) inhabiting a school with no running water and no private sanitation in section 37 of Al-Thawra, while section 76 practically floats over a sewage lake. Some families live in garbage. These places have become key centers of

An Iraqi woman pleads with U.S. troops from the 1st Armored Division to let her get in the line to exchange 10,000 dinar notes at a neighborhood exchange. LYNSEY ADDARIO/CORBIS 2003

organized crime. While the religious parties have succeeded in reducing the number of thefts, there are other uncontrolled crimes, such as the stealing of electric cables and the melting of these cables in open smelting areas, a process that emits black thick smoke and further contaminates the environment.

Given the lack of security, legitimate economic activity has been thwarted, prices have gone up, and gangs have been easily transformed into crime syndicates. Further complicating economic recovery is the absence of a national or even regional telecommunications system: only three out of the nine districts in Baghdad have a working telephone system.

It is not difficult to identify all of these problems, but is it really possible to fully convey the agony of living under occupation?

BAGHDAD JOURNAL #3

One of our visits in Baghdad was to Firdos Square, the famous site where the statue of Saddam Hussein was toppled, a scene that was shown over and over again on U.S. television. Now a new, rather indecipherable three-headed statue by a young Iraqi artist was in its place. But curiously, on the column just beneath the statue, someone had written in bright red paint and in perfect English, "All done. Go home."

Sitting around the circle in the brutal heat were money changers with thick wads of bills with Saddam Hussein on them, which, ironically, is still the currency. Behind the money changers were mounds of barbed wire and U.S. soldiers sitting atop ferocious-looking tanks, weapons readied—a common scene on the streets of Baghdad.

Two elderly money changers in long flowing robes and white caps were sitting at their outdoor stand, and we started chatting. They asked where we were from. "Oh, America," one answered, crossing his arms against his chest, "I love America." "How about the soldiers?" we asked, pointing behind them. The man who "loved America" said how happy they were to be free of Saddam Hussein, but the other man pointed to the column with the graffiti. "So you think the soldiers should go home to America?" I asked. Both men broke out

in big grins. "Yes, Saddam gone. That's good. Soldiers should go, too. Many Iraqis don't like them here."

They told us that if conditions in Iraq did not improve soon, ordinary Iraqis, not fundamentalists, would fight to get rid of the Americans. "We have a nine-thousand-year-old culture, you have a two-hundred-year-old culture," one of the men said, "I think we can figure out our own future."

Iraqis are puzzled why the United States, a country that can make bombs so smart they target a particular building from 30,000 miles in the air, can't give them electricity or create a functioning economy. Some are so puzzled that they have concluded that the United States is purposely trying to destroy every aspect of the economy so that they can come in and rebuild it in their own image. Others attribute the mess to incompetence, arrogance, or stupidity.

No matter the reason, in this land of 120-degree heat and no rain, the U.S. is sinking deeper and deeper into a quagmire. The Iraqis are a patient, generous people. For lack of an alternative, most are still willing to give the U.S. more time, but the clock is ticking, and patience is wearing thin.

Continued . . .

Iraqi women who worked with the Central Bank in Baghdad work at a neighborhood exchange. LYNSEY ADDARIO/CORBIS 2003

American soldiers with the 1st Armored Division. LYNSEY ADDARIO/CORBIS 2003

A PROGRESSIVE MUSLIM CRITIQUE
OF THE U.S. OCCUPATION OF IRAQ

The ongoing U.S. occupation of Iraq presents a special challenge for Muslims who self-identify as socially and politically progressive. The challenge is to speak out, rise up, and act against the unilateral American display of unbridled military power, as well as against acts of violence by some Iraqis toward that same American might or perceived Iraqi sympathizers. This double critique arises out of the Qur'anic view that to save the life of one human being—any human being—is to have saved the life of all humanity, and to take the life of a single human being, any human being, is as if to destroy all of humanity [Qur'an 5:32].

At the heart of a progressive Muslim identity is a simple assumption, the notion that all human life on this planet—Muslim and non-Muslim, female and male, civilian and military, poor or rich, "North" or "South," gay or straight—carries exactly the same intrinsic worth. This essential value of human life is due to the presence of Divine spirit in all of humanity, the same spirit that, according to the Qur'an, God breathed into each and every human being[1] [Qur'an 15:29 and 38:72]. By starting from this premise of the worth and dignity of each and every human life, progressive Muslims move to affirming the sanctity of each human life and the right of each community to a notion of global justice that allows them to realize their vision of prosperity, dignity, and righteousness, as long as that vision does not come at the expense of any other community. We have to be clear about this point: our task is not to "humanize" Iraqis—one can only humanize something that is not already fully human. The Iraqis, exactly like us, already *possess* their full God-given humanity. If we have failed to see and interact with Iraqis on a human level, if we have not listened to their cries, seen their tears, mourned their deaths, it is because they have been presented to us as inhuman, subhuman, or nonhuman.

Progressive Muslims oppose the occupation of Iraq on many fronts. First and foremost, the horrific tactics followed by the Bush administration, including the bombing of heavily populated urban sites, have led to a large number of civilian casualties. Following in the footsteps of Gandhi, Martin Luther King Jr., and the Dalai Lama, we reject this unleashing of violence against the poorest peoples of the earth. The perverse pleasure that the Pentagon and State Department derived from their death fantasy, described as Operation "Shock and Awe," does indeed shock the sensitivity of those who see Iraqis as fellow human beings with hopes and dreams and loves and joys of their own that are every bit as precious as our own. The Bush regime repeatedly attempted to persuade/delude us that this operation would be accurate and precise, that these bombs are very "smart." So-called "smart bombs" used in a mis-guided policy of deliberate cruelty result in nothing short of indiscriminate massacre.

The loss of human life on the Iraqi side affects Muslims powerfully, leading directly to an increase in vehement anti-Americanism all over this world. The American presence

in Iraq, coupled with U.S. support of an Israeli regime bent on brutal oppression of Palestinians and an increasingly Hindu nationalist regime in India which participates in massacres of Muslims in Gujarat and Kashmir: all these lead to a volatile and dangerous rise in hatred of America and Americans all over the world. While many Americans may wish to see ourselves as upholders of freedom and democracy, many people all over the world—and increasingly large numbers of Muslims—see the U.S. as a supporter of many forms of exploitation, domination, and oppression.

Muslims see themselves as part of a grand spiritual community (the *umma*) that stretches from Indonesia to Morocco, from South Africa to the U.S. That the word *umma* is itself derived from the word *"umm,"* meaning "mother," gives an indication of the closeness and spiritual affinity among Muslims of various backgrounds: the bonds of faith are as strong as those shared by the children born to and nurtured by the same mother. It is for this reason that the ongoing wave of Muslim casualties all over the world has been so devastating for American Muslims to bear. The wars in Afghanistan and Iraq have each resulted in civilian casualties far greater than that of September 11, yet the loss of these lives has hardly been engaged by the American media or government with the same humanity that we have treated the loss of American life, both military and civilian. The most accurate estimate of the civilian casualties in Afghanistan comes from Marc Herold, who states that "between 3,125 and 3,620 Afghan civilians were killed between October 7 [2001] and July 31 [2002]."[2] There have also been large-scale casualties in Iraq. The most recent estimate by the Associated Press puts the number of Iraqi civilians who died in the first month of the 2003 war at 3,240.[3] Other independent evaluations of the Iraq casualty count put the number even higher, between 6,139 and 7,849.[4] When pressed to explain such a high number of civilian deaths in a war that was represented as being conducted through "precision targets" and "smart bombs," General Tommy Franks responded: "We don't do body counts." For American Muslims, this callous disregard for Muslim civilians—coupled with the pomp and circumstance that surrounds the rightly joyous occasion of rescuing American prisoners such as Private Jessica Lynch[5]—can only be explained as arising out of the different worth attached to American as opposed to Muslim lives. It is this much resented double standard that Muslims in both this country and beyond see as an unspoken and unjust aspect of American foreign policy.

And yet as progressive Muslims, we cannot and will not limit our engagement simply to the evils of the American government. We have a moral duty to also speak up against the culture of violence that now pervades segments of Iraqi societies, a violence that is unleashed against UN workers, fellow Iraqis, and yes, American soldiers. No just ends can ever be attained through violent and unjust means. The ends are the very fruits of the trees of our means, and the poisoned tree of violence can never lead to delicious fruits of dignity. In addressing American violence before Iraqi violence, I am specifically following in the footsteps of Martin Luther King Jr., who stated: "I knew that I could never again raise my voice against the violence of the oppressed in the ghettos without having first spoken clearly to the greatest purveyor of violence in the world today, my own government." Our task is to do more than condemn: we must work with Iraqis in finding a way to voice their righteous rebellion of resistance—indeed, their *jihad*—against the American occupation in a nonviolent way. This is a great challenge, but I believe that we have no choice but to follow every skillful nonviolent means necessary. (Yes, Buddhist ethics of nonviolence can be combined in Malcolm X-ian urgency in a progressive Muslim agenda.)

It is this simultaneous critique of U.S. military might (disguised as "the coalition") and Iraqi violent outbursts which leaves progressive Muslims in an isolated space in the middle. And yet it is from this space in the middle that we reach out to all of humanity. In doing so we recall the Qur'anic injunction that states that notions of social justice (*'adl*) and spiritual excellence (*ihsan*) are indeed connected. May we bring some healing into this much-fractured world. May that healing begin with you and me, at this very moment.

Amin . . .

1. Omid Safi, "The Times They Are A-Changin'—A Muslim Quest for Justice, Gender Equality, and Pluralism," in *Progressive Muslims: On Justice, Gender, and Pluralism* (Oxford: Oneworld Publications, 2003).

2. Marc Herold is a professor of economics at University of New Hampshire. His data can be accessed at: http://pubpages.unh.edu/~mwherold/AfghanDailyCount.pdf. Also, see http://www.guardian.co.uk/afghanistan/comment/story/0,11447,770999,00.html.

3. http://story.news.yahoo.com/news?tmpl=story&u=/ap/20030610/ap_on_re_mi_ea/iraq_counting_the_dead_7.

4. http://iraqbodycount.net/bodycount.htm [as of September 20, 2003].

5. For initial coverage of this episode, see http://news.bbc.co.uk/2/hi/middle_east/2908477.stm. By now, some of the mythmaking that surrounded this rescue is being reevaluated: www.timesonline.co.uk/article/0,5944-648517,00.html.

PREVIOUS SPREAD: An Iraqi woman walks between rows of bodies, laid out in a building, which were discovered in a mass grave south of Baghdad. LYNSEY ADDARIO/CORBIS 2003

SEEKING HONESTY IN U.S. POLICY

During the Gulf War in 1991, when I was in charge of the American Embassy in Baghdad, I placed a copy of Lewis Carroll's *Alice in Wonderland* on my office coffee table. I thought it conveyed far better than words ever could the weird world that was Iraq at that time, a world in which nothing was what it seemed: The several hundred Western hostages Saddam Hussein took during Desert Shield were not really hostages but "guests." Kuwait was not invaded, but "liberated."

It is clearly time to dust the book off and again display it prominently, only this time because our own government has dragged the country down a rabbit hole, all the while trying to convince the American people that life in newly liberated Iraq is not as distorted as it seems.

It is returning to normal, we are assured, even as we are asked to ante up an additional $75 billion and pressure builds to send more troops and extend the tours of duty of those who are there. Deputy Defense Secretary Paul Wolfowitz tells Congress that all we need is to project a little confidence. The Mad Hatter could not have said it better.

President Bush's speech on Sunday, September 7, was just the latest example of the administration's concerted efforts to misrepresent reality—and rewrite history—to mask its mistakes. The president said Iraq is now the center of our battle against terrorism. But we did not go to Iraq to fight Al-Qaeda, which remains perhaps our deadliest foe, and we will not defeat it there.

By trying to justify the current fight in Iraq as a fight against terrorism, the administration has done two frightening things. It has tried to divert attention from Osama bin Laden, the man responsible for the wave of terrorist attacks against American interests from New York and Washington to Yemen, and who reappeared in rugged terrain in a video broadcast last week. And the policy advanced by the speech is a major step toward creating a dangerous, self-fulfilling prophecy and reflects a fundamental misunderstanding of the facts on the ground.

This is an insurgency we're fighting in Iraq. Our 130,000 soldiers in Iraq now confront an angry but not yet defeated Sunni Muslim population who, although a minority in Iraq, had been in power for a century. We are now also beginning to face terrorists there, but it is our own doing. Our attack on Iraq—and our bungling of the peace—led to the guerrilla insurgency that is drawing jihadists from around the Muslim world. The "shock and awe" campaign so vividly shown on our television screens has galvanized historic Arab envy, jealousy, and resentment of the United States into white-hot hatred of America.

Where once there were thousands, now there are potentially millions of terrorists and sympathizers who will be drawn into this campaign.

We've seen other examples of the kind of insurgency we're now facing. One was in Afghanistan against the Soviets in the 1980s, and we all should know the end of that story by now. Bin Laden was one of the outside jihadists drawn into that battle;

he emerged as the head of a group of hardened soldiers he called "Al-Qaeda."

It is perhaps not surprising that the administration is trying to redefine why we went to Iraq, because we have accomplished so little of what we set out to do—and severely underestimated the commitment it would take to deal with the aftermath of war.

The president told us in his seminal speech in Cincinnati in October 2002 that Iraq "possesses and produces chemical and biological weapons . . . is seeking nuclear weapons . . . has given shelter and support to terrorism, and practices terror against its own people."

He dismissed the concerns raised by critics of his approach as follows: "Some worry that a change of leadership in Iraq could create instability and make the situation worse. The situation could hardly get worse, for world security and for the people of Iraq. The lives of Iraqi citizens would improve dramatically if Saddam Hussein were no longer in power."

Now we know that even if we find chemical or biological weapons, the threat that they posed to our national security was, to be charitable, exaggerated.

It all but disappeared from the president's speech last week, and Defense Secretary Donald Rumsfeld, one of the leading proponents of the threat, now tells us that he didn't even ask the chief weapons-of-mass-destruction sleuth in Iraq, David Kay, for a status report during his recent trip to Baghdad, relegating such weapons to the same dark corner as bin Laden, whose name rarely passes the lips of our leaders these days.

Indeed, in the most telling revision of the justification for going to war, the State Department's undersecretary for arms control, John Bolton, recently said that whether Saddam's government actually possessed weapons of mass destruction "isn't really the issue. The issue, I think, has been the capability that Iraq sought to have . . . WMD programs."

In other words, we're now supposed to believe that we went to war not because Saddam's arsenal of weapons of mass destruction threatened us, but because he had scientists on his payroll.

And the cakewalk postwar scenario that had been painted by some in the administration is anything but. More Americans have died since the president announced the end of major combat operations than during the war itself. The cost runs $1 billion per week in military support alone, and some experts say our deployment is already affecting future military preparedness.

Iraqis live in chaotic conditions as crime flourishes in the unpatrolled streets, and family squabbles are settled vigilante style; basic services such as electricity remain unavailable to large segments of the urban population.

The truth is, the administration has never leveled with the American people on the war with Iraq.

It is true that many people outside the administration, including me and many leading Democrats, thought Saddam had residual stocks of weapons of mass destruction; disarmament was a legitimate international objective supported unanimously by the United Nations Security Council. But we did not need to rush to war before exploring other, less risky options.

Invasion, conquest, and occupation was always the highest-risk, lowest-reward choice. The intrusive UN inspections were disrupting Saddam's programs and weakening him in the eyes of his key supporters, including in the Iraqi military. That would explain why the United States, according to reports, was able to thoroughly infiltrate the army before the onset of hostilities and obtain commitments from Iraqi generals to send their troops home rather than have them fight.

The administration short-circuited the discussion of whether war was necessary because some of its most powerful members felt it was the best option—ostensibly because they had deluded themselves into believing that they could easily impose flowering democracies on the region.

A more cynical reading of the agenda of certain Bush advisers could conclude that the Balkanization of Iraq was always an acceptable outcome, because Israel would then find itself surrounded by small Arab countries worried about each other instead of forming a solid block against Israel. After all, Iraq was an artificial country that had always had a troublesome history.

One way the administration stopped the debate was to oversell its intelligence. I know, because I was in the middle of the efforts to determine whether Iraq had attempted to purchase uranium "yellowcake"—a form of lightly processed ore—from Africa.

At the request of the administration I traveled to the West African nation of Niger in February 2002 to check out the allegation. I reported that such a sale was highly unlikely, but my conclusions—as well as the same conclusions from our ambassador on the scene and from a four-star Marine Corps general—were ignored by the White House.

Instead, the president relied upon an unsubstantiated reference in a British white paper to underpin his argument in the State of the Union address that Saddam was reconstituting his nuclear weapons programs. How many times did we hear the president, vice president, and others speak of the looming threat of an Iraqi mushroom cloud?

Until several months ago, when it came out that the country was Niger, I assumed that the president had been referring to another African country. After I learned, belatedly to be sure, I came forward to insist that the administration correct the misstatements of fact. But the damage had already been done.

The overblown rhetoric about nuclear weapons inspired fear and drowned out the many warnings that invasion would create its own formidable dangers.

Middle East experts warned over and over again that Iraq's many religious and ethnic factions could start battling each other in a bloody struggle for power. Former British foreign secretary Douglas Hurd fretted that we would unleash a terrorist-recruiting bonanza, and former U.S. national security adviser Brent Scowcroft warned of a security meltdown in the region.

The U.S. army's top general at the time, Eric Shinseki, meanwhile, questioned the "cakewalk" scenario. He told Congress that we would need several hundred thousand soldiers in Iraq to put an end to the violence against our troops and against each other. His testimony was quickly repudiated by both Rumsfeld and Wolfowitz.

As we now know, he was close to the mark. Our 130,000 soldiers are failing to stem the violence. Even as Rumsfeld says jauntily that all is going well, Secretary of State Colin Powell is running to the United Nations to try to get more foreign boots on the ground. One of the administration's staunchest supporters, British Foreign Secretary Jack Straw, says ominously that we risk strategic failure if we don't send reinforcements.

And the infighting that Middle East experts feared could still erupt. The majority Shiite Muslim population, brutalized during Saddam's rule, is content with a tactical truce with our forces so long as they are free to consolidate their control and the United States continues to kill Sunni Muslims so that they don't have to. That truce is threatened not only by Shiite political ambition but also by ongoing skirmishes with the Sunnis.

The recent car bomb at the An-Najaf mosque that killed one of Shiite Islam's most influential clerics and head of the largest Shiite party in Iraq almost resulted in the outbreak of civil war between the two groups. Widespread belief that Sunni elements were behind the assassination and that the United States failed in its responsibilities for security has brought Shiite armed militias back onto the streets, actively seeking to avenge the death of their leader. Such a war within a war would make our occupation infinitely more dangerous.

Some now argue that the president's speech Sunday [September 7, 2003] represents a change of course. Even if the administration won't admit it made any mistakes, the mere call for international involvement should be enough to persuade the world to accept the burden of assisting us as we continue to control both the military and the economic reconstruction.

That may well be true, but we cannot count on the international community to do our bidding blindly. While the administration scurries back to the United Nations for help, our historic friends and allies still smart from the gratuitous insults hurled at them nine months ago. This is the same United Nations which Richard Perle, a not-so-invisible hand behind the war, recently called an "abject failure."

As Zbigniew Brzezinski, who was President Carter's national security adviser, has pointed out, at a time when our military might is at its zenith, our political and moral authority is at its lowest ebb. Essential trust has been broken, and it will take time to repair. At a minimum, we need to jettison the hubris that has driven this policy, the pretensions of moral rectitude that mask a jodhpurs-and-pith-helmet imperialism that cannot succeed.

In the meantime, we must demonstrate that we understand that more than military might is required to tame the anger in the region. This includes both the internationalization of the reconstruction effort and the redoubling of efforts to ease tensions on the Israeli-Palestinian front.

That is the thorn that must be pulled from the side of the region. The road to peace in the Middle East still goes through Jerusalem.

But before we can hope to win back international trust or start down a truly new path in Iraq, the administration has to start playing it straight, with the American people and with the world. Recent administration statements, including the president's speech, suggest that it still prefers to live in a fantasy world.

OVERLEAF: An Iraqi man pleads with Lieutenant Colonel Haight of the 82nd Airborne Division after being caught with a gun during a raid on a wedding party after Haight's unit heard gunshots. LYNSEY ADDARIO/CORBIS 2003

BAGHDAD JOURNAL #4

We return to the palace for our meeting with Margaret Bhadi. We've been told by Medea Benjamin that we shouldn't leave the palace without seeing the chapel, so we ask a young Iraqi woman sitting in the entry of Bremer's office where it is.

"I'll take you," Rajaa volunteers. She's an interpreter for the CPA. As we follow her down a very long corridor, we pass men in uniforms who move between offices or sit at tables in the anteroom chambers. The first set of doors she tries is locked; she tries all of them, unsuccessfully, but unperturbed, she continues to the next giant hallway. There is a notice of religious services—Christian, Jewish, and Mormon—posted outside the chapel.

She finds an open door and we enter.

The chapel is huge and clad in marble, with lushly painted murals of missiles and rockets, almost comically phallic, on the walls and ceiling.

We are staggered by the absurdity of it but try not to laugh in her presence.

"We believed in Saddam, and he was taking our money and building this," Rajaa says, the wounds of betrayal obvious in her voice.

She sees our amazement and says, "This is nothing, follow me."

As we walk further down the hall, Rajaa talks about her life in Baghdad during the bombing. For two months she couldn't leave her home because she was too afraid. Now she doesn't care if she lives or dies.

A woman translator sits at the main entrance of the Palace of the Brigade, headquarters of the 1st Armored Division; she does not tell anyone in her neighborhood that she works for coalition forces. LYNSEY ADDARIO/CORBIS 2003

We exit one building and enter another. Huge statues of Saddam still stand atop the palace, four identical images, frightening and intact. This wing of the palace feels empty and vast; it is unoccupied. There are more huge rooms, also decorated with gold and marble and looming images of rockets and missiles, erect and tumescent, streaking across the painted sky. There is more, much more of the same—it's tacky and cold.

Rajaa continues to tell her stories; she can't seem to tell us fast enough, and she seems unafraid of who might be listening. She can't find enough words to describe the bombing, and she starts to cry. Everyone left Baghdad, she says. She wanted her mother to leave, to walk out of the city, but she was too old. She talks about the drugs and the alcohol, how drug use has grown alongside poverty. Guns are available everywhere for less than ten dollars U.S. Criminals freed when Saddam emptied Baghdad's prisons in October 2002 roam the streets. Many ex-policemen who had been fired in a fit of "de-Baathification" after the invasion have formed armed mafias, taking over neighborhoods, stealing, and extorting protection money. Rajaa tells about the kidnapping of two girls—one thirteen, the other fifteen—in her neighborhood. They were returned after ten days, but they'd been raped, so their families threw them out and left them on the street to die. She talks about the dirt and the absence of services—no electricity, garbage heaped in the roads—and how little she cares for her life now. This is what gives her the courage to risk working with the CPA: What difference does it make if her life is in danger because she works for the Americans, when she doesn't care if she lives or dies?

And it *is* dangerous to work for the Americans. Iraqis who do so are branded as traitors, threatened, and sometimes killed, and Moujahdeens have issued *fatwas* against those who work for the occupiers. Rajaa has to hide that she is employed by the CPA, so she takes a taxi from home each day, which eats into her earnings of $10 a day. She has the taxi drop her off far from the CPA so no one will know that she works there. I ask her about the salaries for men vs. women: she says they are the same. An attorney makes $15 and a laborer makes $5, but gender doesn't determine the salary.

"You take the oil and our jobs," she says as she is called back to her work. "You are like Saddam, who made people suffer so that they would follow him, obey him, because they had little choice."

Rajaa returns to her tasks, and Reverend Patricia Ackerman insists on finding the chaplain, which is difficult because he is well hidden. She returns from her conversation with him appalled. He's not very qualified, and he brags childishly about the huge amount of money he is making—six figures, according to him.

I leave to find the intelligence officer. He is pompous and full of himself. He wants to impress me with his knowledge, so words flow at a brisk pace. "Moderates want freedom: they want to taste democracy," he says. I ask him about Iran because he is Iranian, and he responds, "We won't attack Iran because we are changing their government. We are creating a radio show this week to support the students and begin to create the support needed." These programs are happening from his office, he is proud to announce. He continues: "Fear is the foundation of any government, and they will continue the chaos to create the atmosphere to keep their power."

Continued . . .

VEILED AND WORRIED IN BAGHDAD

A single word is on the tight, pencil-lined lips of women here. You'll hear it spoken over lunch at a women's leadership conference in a restaurant off busy Al Nidal Street, in a shade-darkened beauty shop in upscale Mansour, in the ramshackle ghettos of Sadr City. The word is "*himaya*," or "security." With an intensity reminiscent of how they feared Saddam Hussein, women now fear the abduction, rape, and murder that have become rampant here since his regime fell. Life for Iraqi women has been reduced to one need that must be met before anything else can happen.

"Under Saddam we could drive, we could walk down the street until two in the morning," a young designer told me as she bounced her four-year-old daughter on her lap. "Who would have thought the Americans could have made it worse for women? This is liberation?"

In their palace surrounded by armed soldiers, officials from the occupying forces talk about democracy. But in the same cool marble rooms, when one mentions the fears of the majority of Iraq's population, one can hear a representative of the Ministry of the Interior, which oversees the police, say, "We don't do women." What they don't seem to realize is that you can't "do" democracy if you don't "do" women.

In Afghanistan women threw off their *burqas* when American forces arrived. In Baghdad the veils have multiplied, and most women are hiding at home instead of working, studying, or playing a role in reconstructing Iraq. Under Saddam Hussein, crimes against women—or at least ones his son Uday, Iraq's vicious Caligula, did not commit—were relatively rare (though solid statistics for such crimes don't exist). Last October the regime opened the doors to the prisons. Kidnappers, rapists, and murderers were allowed to blend back into society, but they were kept in check by the police state. When the Americans arrived and the police force disappeared, however, these old predators reemerged alongside new ones. And in a country that essentially relies on rumor as its national news, word of sadistic abduction quickly began to spread.

A young Iraqi woman I met represents the reality of these rumors. Sitting in her darkened living room surrounded by female relatives, she leans forward to show the sutures running the length of her scalp. She and her fiancé were carjacked by a gang of thieves in July, and when one tried to rape her, she threw herself out of the speeding car. She says that was the last time she left the house. She hasn't heard a word from her fiancé since he went to the police station to file a report, not about the attempted rape, but about his missing Toyota RAV-4.

"What's important isn't a woman's life here, but a nice car," she said with a blade-sharp laugh.

Two sisters, thirteen and eighteen, weren't as lucky. A neighbor—a kidnapper and murderer who had been released in the general amnesty—led a gang of heavily armed friends to their home one night a few weeks ago. The girls were beaten and raped. When the police finally arrived, the attackers fled with the thirteen-year-old. She was taken to an abandoned house and left there, blindfolded, for a couple of weeks before she was dropped at her door upon threat of death if anyone learned of what had happened. Now she hides out with her sister, young brother, and mother in an abandoned office building in a seedy neighborhood.

"What do you expect?" said the eighteen-year-old. "They let out the criminals. They got rid of the law. Here we are."

Even these brutalized sisters are luckier than many women in Iraq. They have no adult male relatives, and thus are not at risk for the honor killings that claim the lives of many Muslim women here. Tribal custom demands that a designated male kill a female relative who has been raped, and the law allows only a maximum of three years in prison for such a killing, which Iraqis call "washing the scandal."

"We never investigate these cases anyway—someone has to come and confess the killing, which they almost never do," said an investigator, who looked into the case and then dismissed it because the sisters "knew one of the men, so it must not be kidnapping."

This violence has made postwar Iraq a prison of fear for women. "This issue of security is the immediate issue for women now—this horrible time that was triggered the very first day of the invasion," said Yanar Mohammed, the founder of the Organization of Women's Freedom in Iraq.

Ms. Mohammed organized a demonstration against the violence last month. She also sent a letter to the occupation administrator, Paul Bremer, demanding his attention. Weeks later, with no reply from Mr. Bremer, she shook her head in the shadowy light of her office, darkened by one of frequent blackouts here. "We want to be able to talk about other issues, like the separation of mosque and state and the development of

Sunni Iraqi girls pray during Friday afternoon prayer at the Haja Dalal Al-Kubaisi Mosque in Baghdad.
LYNSEY ADDARIO/CORBIS 2003

a civil law based on equality between men and women, but when women can't even leave their homes to discuss such things, our work is quite hard," she said.

Baghdadi women were used to a cosmopolitan city in which doctorates, debating, and dancing into the wee hours were ordinary parts of life. That Baghdad now seems as ancient as this country's Mesopotamian history. College students are staying home; lawyers are avoiding their offices. A formerly first-world capital has become a city where the women have largely vanished.

To support their basic liberties will no doubt require the deeply complicated task of disentangling the threads of tribal, Islamic, and civil law that have made misogyny systemic in each. This is a matter of culture, not just policy.

But to understand the culture of women in Iraq, coalition officials must venture beyond their razor-wired checkpoints and step down from their convoys of Land Cruisers so they can talk to the nation they occupy. On the streets and in the markets, they'll receive warm invitations to share enormous lunches in welcoming homes, as is the Iraqi custom. And there they'll hear this notion repeated frankly and frequently: without *himaya* for women, there will be no place for democracy to grow in Iraq.

American troops stand guard. LYNSEY ADDARIO/CORBIS 2003

ANNE E. BRODSKY and TAHMEENA FARYAL

WOMEN: CANARIES IN THE COAL MINE OF INTERNATIONAL FOREIGN POLICY

The treatment of women by a particular society often renders them canaries in the coal mine, foretelling the prospects for a range of human rights issues from child welfare to freedom of association and dissent. In the current geopolitical climate in which the U.S. and other Western players are exploiting military might while claiming the role of societal liberators, the conditions of women's rights within Afghanistan and Iraq are a reflection not only of the indigenous cultures of the regions, but also of the intervention priorities and goals of the U.S. and its allies.

The speciousness of the assertion that women's rights are at the core of the recent American invasions' goals is revealed when one looks at the conditions on the ground post–U.S. intervention. In Iraq, since the ouster of Saddam Hussein we have heard relatively little about women, and what news is getting out has not been positive. In stark contrast to their conditions under Baath rule, Iraqi women are now wearing veils, staying at home, and avoiding school and work to protect themselves against the estimated twenty daily kidnappings and rapes. Meanwhile, girls' school attendance has dropped by more than 50 percent, honor killings are on the rise, and only three of the twenty-five members of the U.S.- and British-appointed Governing Council are women.[1] Tragically, one member of that underrepresented segment of Iraqi women, Akila al-Hashemi, was assassinated on September 20, 2003.

To get a better sense of what hangs in the balance in Iraq months after U.S. "liberation," one need look no further than Afghanistan. The experiences of Afghan women two years post-Taliban speak volumes about the long-term prospects for the women of Iraq. The women of Afghanistan, as the first "beneficiaries" of an aggressive American anti-terror foreign policy, are the canary's canary.

SUSPICIOUS PRETEXT

After September 11, George W. Bush announced his intention to bomb Afghanistan in retaliation for the Taliban's role in sheltering Osama bin Laden and Al-Qaeda. Both the President and the First Lady co-opted the oppression of Afghan women as a legitimating factor in the overthrow of the Taliban, suspiciously ignoring the fact that Afghan women had already suffered under five years of Taliban rule while the U.S. negotiated for oil pipelines and poppy eradication. Those same women had also suffered under the previous four years of atrocities committed by Jehadi fundamentalists, whose regime was the result of a decision by the U.S., Pakistan, and other Western countries to arm, nurture, and support brutal warlords in an attempt to use Afghans as pawns in the Cold War. These Jehadi warlords, including many that the U.S. coalition returned to power post-Taliban as part of the current Northern Alliance–controlled transitional government, were so brutal towards women (and the entire population) that the Taliban were at first welcomed by the people as liberating heroes. Bush wielded the claim to care about the plight of Afghan women like a convenient sympathy card, one that brought "compassionate conservative" clout to his plan to bomb the same Afghan women he was claiming to liberate. Thus violence and retribution were transformed into chivalrous liberation.

When the Taliban were driven from Kabul, the fawning U.S. press reported euphoria in the streets—people dancing, men shaving their beards and changing into Western clothes, women taking off their *burqas*. A heartwarming picture to be sure, but a closer look at the footage reveals that the jubilant "people" in the streets were mostly men and boys; there were few women to be seen, with *burqas* or without. And as the Northern Alliance marched back into Kabul, bringing back their legacy of oppression and atrocity focused first and foremost on women, Afghan euphoria quickly evaporated as women came to realize that their so-called liberation was nothing more than a PR campaign. The other sad truth facing the Afghan people was the civilian death toll from U.S. bombing, estimated by Marc Herold to be higher than the number who died in the September 11 terrorist attacks in the U.S.[2]

After reports of these glorious promises and joyous victories, however, people in the West assumed that progress had been made and would naturally continue. Afghan women also hoped that some good might come after yet more war, violence, and civilian deaths, but it didn't take long before their hopes were shattered as promises of freedom and opportunity were shown to be implausible in the fundamentalist-controlled reality that is post-Taliban Afghanistan. Meanwhile, in the West it became harder to learn of this reality; the press attention waned, moving on to the military buildup with Iraq, a country with a remarkably similar history of U.S. support through decades of lethal dictatorship.

Now, several years after the Taliban defeat, the realities of life for Afghan women are a world apart from the political and media gloss. As an Afghan man living in Jalalabad told us in June 2003, "The images the West has of Afghanistan now are like looking at the flowers from the horse."

LOYA JIRGA

There was much news of the Loya Jirga, or traditional grand assembly, which was held in June 2002 to elect the transitional government and president to run the country until general elections in June 2004. As set forth at the Bonn meeting the previous winter, the Loya Jirga was to consist of democratically selected representatives from constituencies throughout the country and regional refugee community, with 160 of 1,500 seats reserved for women. Perhaps the most important stipulation was that warlords, criminals, and those guilty of human rights abuses were to be barred from attending.

Ultimately, 200 Afghan women participated in the Loya Jirga, and one woman (now reported to have been propped up by the Northern Alliance warlords who were present in large numbers, having circumvented both the ban on their attendance and the requirement for democratic selection) ran for president. The "reality gap" between what the Loya Jirga promised and what it eventually delivered is best explained by Belquis Ahmadi, Afghanistan program coordinator for the International Human Rights Law Group and a delegate to the Loya Jirga herself:

Afghan women emerged from the Loya Jirga facing not only the discrimi-

Afghan women dress in *burqas* so they may leave the house. LYNSEY ADDARIO/CORBIS

nation and harassment that are a part of Afghan life, but a real danger to their physical security. Those who pose these threats to Afghan women are no longer international pariahs (the Taliban) but participants in the heralded new government of Afghanistan. When I first entered the Loya Jirga, I was inspired by the outspokenness of the Afghan men and women in attendance. Many women found the courage to deliver speeches before the mostly male crowd, campaign for candidates and even make efforts to confront the warlords who were there. One Afghan woman even pursued a largely symbolic run for the presidency. But such apparent signs of progress were eclipsed by a growing sense of futility in the face of threats, bribes, and intimidation by warlords and their supporters.[3]

In what could be a preview of similar tragedies in Iraq, Afghan women's further participation in the government since the Loya Jirga has been quite limited, with only two of twenty-six ministerial positions given to women by President Karzai, and very few women holding jobs in the government at all outside of the Ministry for Women's Affairs. Even that newly created ministry, focusing exclusively on women, is a mixed blessing; on the one hand, it demonstrates the importance of women's issues for the country, but on the other hand, according to Habiba Sorabi, the Women's Minister, it leads inexorably to their marginalization. Other ministries act as though they do not need to bother themselves with any issues of gender since it is believed that the underfunded and disparaged Women's Ministry can somehow do it all.[4]

ELUSIVE SECURITY

In two reports on the situation in Afghanistan, Human Rights Watch has not minced words:[5]

The situation today—widespread insecurity and human rights abuse—was not inevitable, nor was it the result of natural or unstoppable social or political forces in Afghanistan. It is, in large part, the result of decisions, acts, and omissions of the United States (U.S.) government, the governments of other coalition members, and parts of the transitional Afghan government itself. The warlords themselves, of course, are ultimately to blame. . . . A number of serious consequences flow from the security problems and impunity documented in this report. . . . Targeting of women and girls by police and soldiers on the streets not only impairs their liberty of movement, but also has the effect of restricting their access to education, health care, and jobs, and keeps many from participating in Afghanistan's political and civic life and reconstruction.[6]

As reported both by Human Rights Watch and to us during interviews conducted in Afghanistan in the summer of 2003, harassment, threats of kidnapping, rape, forced marriage, and other violence continue to severely limit the lives of women and girls. *Burqas* are still ubiquitous on the streets, not due to the freely chosen expression of religious convictions, but rather due to fear and threat. Fear causes families to limit women's and girl's access to life and resources outside of the home to the extent that even those families who believe in greater freedoms for women are forced to behave in ways that promote and condone the same restrictions imposed by the Taliban. Meanwhile, Afghan women, fearing to venture from their homes, opt to restrict their own activities. And this is by no means an isolated outcome; Iraq is currently in the throes of the same lamentable chaos. As Lauren Sandler wrote recently in the *New York Times*:

> Under Saddam Hussein, crimes against women—or at least ones his son Uday, Iraq's vicious Caligula, did not commit—were relatively rare. . . . Last October, the regime opened the doors to the prisons. Kidnappers, rapists, and murderers were allowed to blend back into society, but they were kept in check by the police state. When the Americans arrived and the police force disappeared, however, these old predators reemerged alongside new ones. And in a country that essentially relies on rumor as its national news, word of sadistic abduction quickly began to spread. . . . This violence has made postwar Iraq a prison of fear for women. "This issue of security is the immediate issue for women now—this horrible time that was triggered the very first day of the invasion," said Yanar Mohammed, the founder of the Organization of Women's Freedom in Iraq.[7]

While this rampant instability is damaging to any woman's life, whether in Iraq or in Afghanistan, it is devastating for those who are breadwinners for families decimated by years of war and loss. In the case of Afghanistan, the security force—4,800 International Security Assistance Force (ISAF) peacekeepers limited to Kabul only—is simply too small and localized to make a real difference. Its ratio of 1 peacekeeper to every 5,555 Afghans, versus the 1-to-65 ratio in Bosnia after its war, is the result of repeated U.S. opposition to an expansion requested by President Karzai, humanitarian groups, and the Afghan people.[8]

If nothing changes, it is impossible to fathom that the same women and families who are too afraid to allow their female relatives to go to a market will be convinced to allow them to leave the house to vote in the 2004 elections. This is just one way in which the current lack of security makes the prospect of free and fair elections in the supposedly democratic and liberated Afghanistan—to say nothing of Iraq—a myth. Further, the threats, harassment, arrests, and death sentences facing Afghan journalists who speak out against the current government (and especially against elements of the Northern Alliance) make public dissent a life-or-death decision, effectively silencing all but the most stalwart or underground of voices for democracy, security, peace, and freedom.[9]

This is yet another sad omen for the people of Iraq. The political voice of the people, expressed in the form of free electoral debate and participation, doesn't stand much of a chance in a climate of fear and violence.

SCHOOLS UNDER SIEGE

When schools and universities were reopened for Afghans of both genders in March 2002, it marked the end of a five-year ban on girls' and women's education. While many, especially in the urban centers of Afghanistan, have joyously returned to schools, only 32 percent of the 3.6 million students currently attending schools are girls.[10] Further, the 4,000 open schools, which operate double and triple sessions each day, are inadequate, leaving another (conservatively) estimated one million school-age children, the vast majority of whom are girls, out of school.[11]

With a literacy rate generously estimated at 16 percent for women over the age of fifteen,[12] there is no doubt that education should be a first priority for building an Afghanistan—and Iraq—in which women can participate. It is not just a lack of physical schools which keeps girls from education: in the first six months after girls' schools reopened, nearly one dozen schools in five provinces were firebombed or otherwise attacked. Further, countless families and teachers throughout Afghanistan have been harassed and threatened for seeking and supporting girls' education.

In addition to the aforementioned general security concerns that confine women to their homes and the specific threats against the education of girls, many girls we talked to during the summer of 2003—they were attending literacy classes run by the Revolutionary Association of the Women of Afghanistan (RAWA) instead of government schools—offered the following reasons for not being back in Afghan schools:
   * Lack of support from their families for education.
   * Being too old to attend first grade, even though after five years without school this is their proper academic placement.
   * Being too embarrassed to attend class with much younger girls.
   * Having been married young (either by force or by family pressure) and thus being officially banned from attending school with unmarried girls.

The end result, currently visible in Iraq as well as Afghanistan, is an overall decrease in the proportion of girls in school over the past eighteen months.[13]

CIVIL RIGHTS IN JEOPARDY

While the entire country waits for the first draft of the new Afghan constitution, months late in its release for comment, the 1964 Constitution is responsible for protecting the rule of law and civil society. Yet neither this nor Afghanistan's 1980 signature to the United Nations' Convention on the Elimination of All Forms of Discrimination Against Women (CEDAW) and the current government recommitment in March 2003 has protected women.

Among other civil rights abuses, women and their children continue to be imprisoned (as they were under the Taliban) for such crimes as attempting to marry a man of their choice, refusing an arranged marriage, leaving abusive husbands, or remarrying after divorce (they are even sometimes accused by the ex-husband of still being married).[14] Meanwhile, in Herat, a western province controlled by warlord Ismail Khan, unmarried girls who are seen with unrelated men are being picked up by the police and forced to undergo physical "chastity checks" at local hospitals.[15]

Remarkably, in the face of all of the broken promises and failures of "liberation," there are Afghans, particularly Afghan women, who have shown amazing resilience and resolve to struggle until a truly free, peaceful, democratic Afghanistan rises from the ashes. The women and men who wage this nonviolent battle today are many of the same who struggled tirelessly against Taliban and Jehadi oppressions, as well as against the Soviet invaders. One example of this resilience is RAWA, which still functions as an underground organization dedicated to provide medical, educational, reconstruction, political, and income-generating aid to Afghans. Even as the world once again forgets about Afghanistan and money is becoming scarce, RAWA continues to provide services that the government and international community promised but which rarely reach ordinary people. RAWA members—outspoken critics of fundamentalist crimes and advocates of secular democracy and freedom, human, and women's rights—

remain at high risk in a country still controlled by armed warlords. Intimidation of shopkeepers who sell RAWA publications, an attack on RAWA's openly run Malalai hospital in Pakistan, and continued threats that arrive through email and phone calls all demonstrate that Afghanistan, to say nothing of Iraq, is still not safe enough for an independent, democratic, humanitarian, and political women's organization.

Another example of Afghan women's resistance is Shakeela, a Hazara educator in Kabul who manages an independent underground school for girls and who once marched fearlessly to Taliban headquarters to demand the release of her falsely imprisoned brother and other men from her community. Even under the Taliban, Shakeela advocated democracy, freedom, and women's rights, and she condemned the atrocities of fundamentalists and warlords, including those from her own ethnic group. While her activism and bravery won her the support of the community, which elected her as their representative (not their female representative, but their community representative) to the 2002 Loya Jirga, her outspoken condemnation of fundamentalism has made her grave enemies among the warlords and their followers. Despite their threats and a lack of financial support (the billions of dollars in international aid money that never make it to the neediest), she directs an Education Center

Three sisters stand in front of their house in a village ruled by Komala Islami, an Islamic extremist group, in northern Iraq.
LYNSEY ADDARIO/CORBIS 2003

that teaches math, science, English, and computer and tailoring skills to Afghan girls, boys, and women. The school, run with the help of an indigenous Afghan women's group, stands as a testament to her fortitude as well as to that of so many Afghan women and men who struggle in similar ways around the country.

While the strength and resilience of the common people of Afghanistan should not be overlooked, it is no excuse for standing back and allowing terrible circumstances, many of which are the making of the U.S. and its allies, to continue. It is tragic to think of how much farther this strength and resilience could have moved the rebuilding of Afghanistan if people were working from an even playing field rather than struggling to dig themselves out of a hole created by the reempowerment of fundamentalist warlords.

REALITY CHECK

Given the realities of life in Afghanistan and Iraq, it is no wonder that the U.S. administration and mainstream press, recalling the comments of the Afghan man from Jalalabad, don't get off the proverbial "liberation" PR horse and look more closely at the flowers. Afghan women traditionally have been and continue to be the unfortunate canaries in this foreign policy coal mine. Witnessing the true conditions of Afghan women calls into question the possibilities for any better outcome in Iraq. Unfortunately, the dangers for Afghan and Iraqi women, as well as all the citizens of both countries who demand freedom, democracy, and human rights, are not just found in the present but in the future as well. When the United States and its allies' claims of peace and democracy are shown to be façades, their actions provide fuel for oppressive groups and ideologies that breed repression, violence, hatred, and terrorism, with the end result perhaps being a similar backlash to that which nurtured the likes of Osama bin Laden and replaced the criminal Jehadis of the Northern Alliance with the Taliban in 1996. Further, when Afghan and Iraqi women are not empowered as active leaders in the physical, social, and legislative rebuilding of their countries, they stand little chance of creating institutions, structures, and mechanisms grounded in the indigenous cultural understandings necessary to advance women's lives in meaningful and lasting ways.

The lessons of Afghanistan do not apply solely to Iraq and other countries that lie in the path of an aggressive U.S. foreign policy, but also to the deteriorating state of democracy and civil liberties in the U.S. itself. And just as the women of Iraq and Afghanistan do not have the luxury of inaction, neither do informed people throughout the world. There is plenty that the average person in the West can do to support the struggle of Afghan and Iraqi women for true democracy and human rights, including:

* Seek alternative sources of information. The World Wide Web is replete with links to independent Western and regional media links, including RAWA,[16] Alternet, Counterpunch, *The Nation*. European left-leaning publications like *The Guardian* report what the *New York Times* doesn't dare. Even the BBC, Reuters, and AFP offer news that you'll never find in the *Washington Post* or the Associated Press.
* Share this information by educating others, writing letters to the editor, and demanding that mainstream press also cover this ongoing crisis.
* Lobby the administration and Congress to demand that the number and location of international peacekeepers in Afghanistan be expanded and that the security of women becomes a top priority.
* Protect democracy and civil rights abroad and in the U.S. by getting involved in the 2004 presidential election. Volunteer for a candidate, register voters, educate voters, but most importantly, VOTE.
* Support the efforts of indigenous women's organizations like RAWA by con-

tributing financially to their humanitarian and political activities.

In this truly global village, where decisions made in Washington and London have life-and-death consequences for people in Kabul and Baghdad—and decisions made in the mountains of Tora Bora have life-and-death consequences in New York City and Bali—all of us, as citizens whose governments are acting in our name, need to act now. As the late Congresswoman Barbara Jordan said in 1977: "The stakes . . . are too high for government to be a spectator sport."[17]

NOTES

1. Susan Milligan, "In Postwar Iraq, Women Lead a Life of Fear," *International Herald Tribune* online, 22 August 2003. Available at http://www.iht.com/articles/107336.htm.

2. Afghanistan's Civilian Deaths Mount," BBC News, 3 January 2003. Available at http://news.bbc.co.uk/I/hi/world/south_asia/1740538.stm.

3. Belquis Ahmadi, "Reality Gap in Afghanistan: Despite Rosy Reports, Women's Rights Remain Wishful Thinking," *Washington Post*, 8 July 2003, A17.

4. Minister Habiba Sorabi, conversation with the authors, Kabul, June 2003.

5. "'Killing You Is a Very Easy Thing for Us': Human Rights Abuses in Southeast Afghanistan," Human Rights Watch, July 2003; "'All Our Hopes Are Crushed': Violence and Repression in Western Afghanistan," Human Rights Watch, October 2002. Available at http://www.hrw.org.

6. Human Rights Watch, July 2003.

7. Lauren Sandler, "Veiled and Worried in Baghdad," *New York Times*, 16 September 2003.

8. "CARE Says Ideal Time to Expand ISAF Mandate in Afghanistan," CARE USA, August 2003. Available at http//:www.careusa.org/newsroom/pressreleases/2003/aug/08112003_afghanistan.asp.

9. "'Killing You Is a Very Easy Thing for Us.'"

10. Ibid.

11. "Taking Stock Update: Afghan Women and Girls Sixteen Months On," Womankind Worldwide, April 2003.

12. Ibid.

13. Isabel Hilton, "Now We Pay the Warlords to Tyrannise the Afghan People: The Taliban Fell But—Thanks to Coalition Policy—Things Did Not Get Better," *The Guardian*, 31 July 2003.

14. Farnaz Fassihi, "Little Has Changed for Wives of Afghan Officials, Rural Women," Newhouse News Service, October 2002; Robyn Dixon, "Rights: Despite Western Pressure for Greater Attention, Many Laws Have Not Changed Since the Taliban Left, and Jails Are Refilling," *Baltimore Sun*, 27 July 2002; Amy Waldman, "Fifteen Women Await Justice in Kabul Prison," *New York Times*, 16 March 2003.

15. "'All Our Hopes Are Crushed.'"

16. The Revolutionary Association of the Women of Afghanistan's website: www.rawa.org.

17. As quoted in Rosalie Maggio, ed., *The Beacon Book of Quotations by Women* (Boston: Beacon Press), p. 141.

BAGHDAD JOURNAL #5

On the bus to the palace we meet an American lieutenant who was working with the United States Agency for International Development (USAID). His job involved uncovering mass graves. He had been taking Iraqi women to the graves, and he told us he felt inadequate to deal with their extreme grief and asked if we might know of any Iraqi women who could help.

to the governing counsel. She described what it was like to start from scratch. Women hold strong positions in all levels of Iraqi life—they are always the number two and three in a ministry or in other governing positions—so qualified was not the problem. The problem was the lack of civic organizations and thus no civic leaders. "Many of the strong women were still locked in their houses or staying home

An Iraqi woman weeps before American troops at a mass grave site as hundreds of bodies are pulled out of the earth.
LYNSEY ADDARIO/CORBIS 2003

We were more than an hour late arriving for our meeting with Margaret Bhadi—things move very slowly in the heat—and she had very little time left for us. The CPA is made up of members of the coalition of the willing: she came from England to advise on gender issues, and her task was to find women to appoint

with their children," she said. The task was made more complicated by the problems with communication tools: without a phone you have to drive to the person's house, or find them at church—which is where she started, in the churches, joining the circle of women after a service to learn who had influence. Over the past month she had found about eighty women to invite to a conference later in the week. The conference had originally been the dream of an Iraqi woman in England, but Paul Bremer heard of her plans and stopped that conference in order to hold his own meeting, which he could control. Margaret complained that the speed with which the conference was being planned hampered her ability to do the job correctly. We could read between the lines and detect the tension between the CPA and the UN: the United Nations Development Fund for Women (UNIFEM) was planning a similar gathering in August with three hundred women. (Two days before the UNIFEM meeting, it was canceled because of the bombing of the UN in Baghdad.)

We asked Margaret the question we'd been asked that morning: Are there women who can help each other deal with the grief they experience at the mass graves? "There's this woman I met, Yanar Mohammed," she told us. She characterized Yanar as an activist and controversial figure. Yanar Mohammed founded the Organization of Women's Freedom in Iraq, an advocacy group addressing women's issues in general, and the problem of honor killings specifically. We asked Margaret if Yanar was among the eighty women participating— no, she is too uncontrollable.

Yanar Mohammed has dedicated herself to fighting injustice and saving women who are in danger of being killed in the name of honor, and her work has made her a target of fundamentalists of all sorts. Religious fundamentalism, having been held somewhat in check by Saddam's secular regime, is rising with a fervor that threatens the already shaky status of Iraqi women, particularly as the long-repressed Shia Muslim majority asserts itself with calls for Islamic rule.

Honor killings are increasing, as are rape and prostitution. Iraq, in many ways, is still a tribal society, and a woman who has sex outside of her marriage—regardless of whether with a lover or due to a rape—is seen as having dishonored the tribe. The only way to restore honor is for the woman to be killed by her male relatives. This practice was legalized by Saddam towards the end of his regime in an effort to shore up support amongst the tribes.

We heard one story about a prominent Iman who preached that no girls should be educated past the sixth grade. Supposedly a man raised his hand and asked, "If my wife is pregnant, should she see a man or a woman doctor?"

"A woman," the Iman pronounced.

"How will there be women doctors if girls don't go to school past the sixth grade?" asked the man.

The Iman had no good answer for that, and the man was later beaten for embarrassing the Iman.

Yanar continues her work in the face of such attitudes. I worry constantly about her safety. "A woman's freedom is the standard of a society's freedom," Yanar said at the end of one of our meetings.

Continued . . .

Iraqi men and women gather at a mass grave site.
LYNSEY ADDARIO/CORBIS 2003

Zakiya Abd weeps as she discusses her daughter's disappearance. LYNSEY ADDARIO/CORBIS 2003

THE PLIGHT OF WOMEN IN IRAQ: BETWEEN U.S. INVASION AND POLITICAL ISLAMIC OPPRESSION

Yanar Mohammed, founder of the Organization of Women's Freedom in Iraq and editor in chief of the newspaper Al Mousawat *(Equality), is a radical defender of women's rights in Iraq. She was interviewed by Medea Benjamin in Baghdad in July 2003.*

For the last thirty-five years, women have been oppressed by the Baathist regime. The previous achievements we in the women's movement attained were aborted, one after another. By the end of the Baathist regime, all the amendments that had been made to our civil law to improve the situation of women were reversed. In the 1990s Saddam Hussein introduced an amendment to the civil law that supported honor killings: the males in families were allowed to kill any female relative they believed brought dishonor to the family. During the 1990s, approximately five thousand women were killed in the northern part of Iraq—and some of those killings were organized by the ruling party.

We have major issues to confront. Women are not considered to be an equal part of humanity, so we are banding together. We are setting up this women's organization, and we will speak out against all the atrocities that are being committed against us as a gender. We will also address the political agendas that aim to keep women in an inferior status in this society.

Our organization works on many levels, but we start with the women who have nobody to speak for them. Though we only began to organize at the end of the war, we have many members. We have women who were fired from their jobs for a variety of reasons. We have women who have no one else to defend them, who were left by their husbands, who have many children to support. We have women who are at risk for honor killings or are suffering from domestic abuse. For some of these cases, we provide a safe haven within our headquarters, but unfortunately we don't have much space, so we can only accommodate a few.

But we've noticed dramatic changes in the women we have been able to shelter. For example, Fatima, who is staying with us, suffered domestic abuse. When she first left her home and came here, she was very shaken. She wore the veil and very concealing clothing; it was as if she were hiding under them. And nobody ever heard her voice. Now the veil is off, she is an outspoken activist, and she believes in the unlimited rights of women. She participated in a demonstration the other day, shouting with everyone else.

This is just one case, and it's just the beginning. I can see millions of women making such progress. Fatima, who had to leave school at an early age, now plans to go back to school; she will find a job, and we will help her establish a good life for herself.

Providing this type of support is the primary mandate of our organization. In addition, many of us who founded the organization have a socialist political vision that sees women in decision-making positions. We do not believe that gaining equal rights is possible if women are not also decision makers. Because of the consecutive wars fought in Iraq, 60 percent of our current population is women. With all of the soldiers that were killed, there are many women with no men to support them; social insurance for them is one big issue that we will be fighting for. We would also like to provide women with language and computer lessons so that they will be more employable. This is the first stage, establishing the organization and offering these services.

The second stage will be to set up a shelter in Baghdad where we can offer an alternative for women who are under immediate threat of honor killings. This is a big and ambitious project, and a dangerous one for us activists, but we are very serious about it, especially since we have previous experience in the north of Iraq, where many of us were members of a group called the Independent Women's Organization. This group set up a shelter for women, and all in all they saved almost four hundred women from honor killings. We housed seventy of these women for quite some time until we were confident that their relatives would not kill them. For the few cases where we could not provide the women with adequate security, we smuggled them out through Turkey and applied to the United Nations to have them taken to Europe, America, and other safe places.

So those are some of our success stories. We have high hopes to be able to do the same here in Baghdad—I'm getting reports from all over the city about honor killings, about domestic abuse. It's getting worse and worse.

Our main struggle here is against political Islam. We think that every person should have freedom of religion or atheism, but for a group of people to oppress and dictate to women that they must wear the veil [*hijab*], to go into the schools and give the orders that all girls should be veiled—this is not right. These people even harass women on the streets if they don't wear the full veil—"full" as in having a piece of black cloth covering your entire body. This is not a humane way for women in the third millennium to be living. These political Islamists should be stopped.

Our vision of the future is one where there will be institutions that protect and advance the rights of women. There must be an institution that reaches into every neighborhood, every house, a sort of human rights watch that looks after the life of every woman. And this institution should be local. This institution, as well as the constitution, must be based on full equality between men and women.

Our biggest battle now is the constitution. Our organization's founding statement puts the constitution in the forefront of our agenda, along with counseling against the compulsory *hijab*, canceling sexual apartheid in schools, and eliminating all articles in the law which are discriminatory against women—especially article 409 in the Civil Law 111, which supports honor killings and lets the murderers go free.

When people say that women always fight for women's rights, I say that is not true. You need egalitarian *people*; you need people who fully believe in freedom and in humanity. Those are the defenders of women. They could be men, they could be women. We have found that some of the honor killings were executed at the hands of women who were following the dominant male belief that women should be kept inferior and that they should follow the rules of patriarchy, which keep women submissive in a society.

When the Americans say that they have a number of women at the forefront working for the future of Iraq, I say that it's not enough. If their policies are not women-friendly, then the two women that I see on the governing council will not advance the cause of women anywhere. We need both women-friendly policies and real representation on these councils.

Regarding the occupation, we were against this notion of the "liberation" of Iraq, which we thought of as a big lie. While it is true that we wanted to get rid of Saddam, destroying our cities and killing our people is not the way to liberate us. This inhuman way of changing the political situation here rests in the belief that killing thousands of people is a fair-enough price for political change. Would George W. Bush accept that even five American people be killed in order to change a bad political regime in the United States? I don't think so. For him, however, the lives of tens of thousands of Iraqis was an acceptable price. This was the first reason that we did not support the current occupation.

The second reason was that we knew there would be a large political vacuum

An Iraqi woman stands off to the side as United States troops from the 1st Armored Division patrol.
LYNSEY ADDARIO/CORBIS 2003

as a result. The Baathists ruled internally for thirty-five years. We feared that after their removal, chaos would ensue and atrocities would occur—and that is exactly what we are seeing these days. Hundreds of women have been raped. In general, people are living with insecurity. They do not have hope for a good future. This feeling of hopelessness is getting stronger and stronger with each passing day with no electricity, no income, no water, no services. We find it unacceptable that we have had to live without electricity for months and months now. We are convinced that this idea of liberation is a big lie.

The occupation setting is really very scary for women. There are many people

Iraqi women. LYNSEY ADDARIO/CORBIS 2003

carrying out revenge killings against the previous Baath regime and its supporters. They are also committing rape, or even group rape, on the daughters of members of the former Baath regime as another tool of political revenge. We heard about a rape that happened in the city of Mosul, where a group sought to kill a Baath official. When he fled, they raped all nine of his daughters and left them; when the other members of their family came and found them raped, honor killings were enforced. Those nine girls were killed on the spot.

We have no protection. We are trapped between the unleashed dark forces of political Islam and tribal culture—both are anti-woman. These two terrible forces were unleashed by the occupying powers, and they have been given credibility to participate in the future agenda of political rule in Iraq. The tribes have been given seats and validation as if they have some legitimate political agenda. They call for the return of an ancient lifestyle where patriarchal structures are dominant and women have no worth. Saddam gave them power in the last year of his rule, providing them with financial support in order to gain their military support, and the tribes grew stronger as a consequence. But now, to our surprise, the occupying troops are also defending them, meeting with them, giving them importance. I see Bremer dancing their tribal dances with them, but I don't hear him talking much about women's rights.

And when the Coalition Provisional Authority created various women's groups, they spoke only to professional women, women who have reached a position in society where they no longer think about honor killings or the single women with no access to employmemt or social insurance because they are out of the poverty cycle—they're outside the circle where women are still oppressed. These are the women with whom Bremer's officials are meeting.

We see a very frightful future, with Iraq becoming a bourgeois society where 5 percent of people in Iraq will be very rich and the other 95 percent will be living in poverty. I walk the streets, and I see groups of young people going in and out of buildings, stealing. Why would they do that in a country that's so rich? It's because they have no social insurance, no work, no opportunity to attend school. They go to bed hungry.

My biggest fear is that the Iraqi people will be dragged through more misery than they can take. The thirteen years of sanctions they've already endured have drained them.

The Organization of Women's Freedom in Iraq calls for the immediate departure of the occupying forces and their immediate replacement by United Nations peacekeepers, who are better trained to deal with postwar situations, especially from a humanitarian point of view. The distribution of food, talking to people at the neighborhood level, dealing with individual families—the UN is more qualified to perform these services than military troops. The military can point guns at people, can kill, can drop bombs here and there, but defending a woman who is in danger of rape or providing food rations to a neighborhood: these are things that the peacekeeping forces of the UN and their organizations can do.

If they come.

Al-Muajaha
The Iraqi Witness
Vol. 1 Issue 3   18 June 2003
www.almuajaha.com
An Independent Weekly Newspaper

RAPE!
New Violence in the New Iraq
9 Year Old Child A Victim

An Al-Muajaha a Special Report

Staff Writers Salaam Al-Jubouri, Salam Al-Onaibi, Hiba Alsoudani, Luith Hadithi, Yasser Hani, Saad Isaam, Hamsa Mohammed, and Waleed Rabi'a all contributed to this report. (The names of victims have been changed for this article)

On 27 May at 4pm, a short man of average build put a gun to Warda Ali's head, dragged her off the street and into an abandoned government building, threw her face down on the ground and brutally raped her. This may unfortunately be a common crime in Iraq now, but what is different is that Warda is only 9 years old.

The failures to restore security or communications in the new Iraq have fueled rampant rumors about girls being kidnapped from their homes or from school or off the street. Sometimes the rumors say that the criminals are those released by Saddam in the amnesty last October. Sometimes the rumors involve foreigners, such as Kuwaitis, who allegedly kidnap Iraqi girls as slaves or to work in brothels inside or outside Iraq. Trying to track down these rumors becomes an endless chase from person to person, each referring you to another friend of a friend who these crimes supposedly happened to. Women rarely leave their homes unaccompanied now, and many parents are frightened to let their daughters out of the house - even to attend school.

Rumors run wild in Baghdad, and as long as Iraq has no government or functioning police force, there is no one keeping statistics on the increase in crimes, including rape. Hospitals deny that they are treating any rape cases, and, despite increased patrols of girls schools and neighborhoods, the police complain that they are unable to deal with the problem. While hard information about the general situation in Baghdad is impossible to discover, individual cases can be verified. Female patients at Al-Rashad Psychiatric Hospital were raped by [Continued on Page 5]

Practicing Freedom
Iraqis Protest Hilla Mayor

By Salam Talib Al-Onaibi

In previous issues of Al-Muajaha we followed the story of the people of Za'faraniia and their message to US President Bush about civilian deaths in their neighborhood due to the explosion of a munitions dump located there, and we also covered the story of students forcing the resignation of Dr. Alim Yacoub from his position as Dean of Mustanseriya Univ ersity's Medi cal College because of his past association with the Ba'ath regime. In this issue we are exploring the most serious case of "practicing freedom" as we travel along this new path of democracy in Iraq: the struggle of the people of Hilla to force the resignation of their new "mayor."

With the fall of the previous government, many individuals have "appointed" themselves into positions of power. In Baghdad, Mohammed Mehson Zubeidi, who is associated with Ahmed Chalabi's Iraqi National Congress, declared himself as the new mayor and attempted to exert the powers of such a position until the US military arrested him and sent him to Doha Base for a brief vacation. People such as this are taking advantage of the current power vacuum throughout Iraq, and when US troops entered Babylon, or Hilla - the "second city" of Iraq - the situation was no different.

"These people don't represent the city because they are just a few thousand."

In Babylon, the mayor today is Iskander Witwit. Though he comes from a respected, religious family in the area, which has a long history of fighting Saddam's regime, Iskander himself was a general in the former Iraqi military. He received so many medals during his career, that he was called a "friend of Saddam." He was also awarded a medal from the Ba'ath Party signifying that he had spent 25 years as a member of that party. This information is confirmed by a hand-written affidavit in Al-Muajaha's possession that was submitted by General Iskander during a court case in Hilla in 2002.

Strangely, "Mayor" Iskander's office manager, Saleem Abdel Mutaleb Beigan, told the press that, his place as mayor when Mohammed Mehson Zubeidi sent one of his assistants, Jowdat Kadham Al-Obaidi, to put a mayor in Babylon 4 days after the fall of Baghdad." One of Iskander's first actions was appointing mayors for towns throughout the area, such as placing Abdel Hussein Alawi as mayor of Mahouweel, a mid-sized town outside Hilla. This process was called a "vote" by Iskander, despite the fact that no vote too actually took place, and all the new mayors were summarily chosen by Iskander from officers in the former Iraqi army who did not do well under Saddam's reign.

According to [Continued on Page 2]

A Burning Question
Who's Helping Baghdad's

By Salaam Al-Jubouri

Baghdad hospitals are suffering from severe shortages in many aspects. They are supposed to be places to recover from disease and injury, but have they become useless? Al-Muajaha visited various hospitals to understand how difficult the situation is today, and get the real story.

After the collapse of medical services during the war, and the massive lootings immediately afterwards, Al-Kindi hospital now has two American tanks and some soldiers protecting the grounds. The gate is surrounded with razor wire. The hospital serves a poor neighbourhood, and is crowded with patients. People now enter the hospital through the emergency section, and injured patients are in full view of everyone entering.

Picture the scene: two ambulances pulled in very fast to the front of Al-Kindi and four patients were carried out on stretchers. The ambulance drivers informed Al-Muajaha that the men had been in an explosion. Six men were seriously burnt from munitions stored in a house. They had been driven more than 600 kilometres from Al-Rutba, a town near the Jordanian border with Iraq. The local hospital in this isolated area is no longer functional, after being bombed during the war.

The patients lay in the hospital for a while. No one tried to treat them at first, until a nurse started cover them in cream. They were horribly burnt. The strong stench of charred flesh was in the air, and you could hardly recognise two of them as people.

Dr. Ali Acka'ab, a resident doctor at Al Kindi told us, "We have no place for these men. All the Burn Units are full, so we have to move them to another hospital."

Al-Muajaha was informed that three men were moved to Al-Karama hospital for treatment, however, on visiting this hospital Al-Muajaha was told the men would also not be able to stay there and would be transferred to a third hospital.

Dr. Belal Al-Rowei, a resident doctor at Al-Karama said, "The Burn Unit in Al-Karama is occupied, we only have space for twelve people. We will transfer these men... to Al-Karkh hospital"

As darkness fell Al-Muajaha drove back to find the ambulances with the burn patients trying to find a place for treatment, Al-Muajaha witnessed one ambulance that was stopped by the American army and the driver was being questioned. A few days later Al-Muajaha continued this enquiry into the fate of these men.

No US troops guard the entrance to Al-Karkh hospital. Security consists [Continued on Page 2]

Baghdad's Merciless Streets
The Problems of Street Children in Iraq

By Amar Hasan Arebge and Nuha Atiya

Hundreds of children are wandering daily in the streets of Baghdad, the city named as the Home of Peace, looking for food, shelter and someone to care for them. They possess a hunger for love and the necessities of life that they couldn't find in the era of Dicatorism, and which is still not found in the new, Freedom era. This article is the second of a continuing series focusing on the problem of Iraq's forgotten street children.

Many of the street children in Baghdad have homes and families they live with. They work in the streets begging or selling small things, such as chewing gum or candy, in order to support their families. Others have neither families nor homes, and they sleep in the streets as well as work in them. Many older children come to Baghdad from other areas in Iraq in the belief that they will find jobs and money. Life for all these children is hard and merciless.

"Ali," a 7 year old street child, was arrested by Iraqi police a week after the war ended, and taken to Al-Rahma Orphanage (the House of Mercy) - despite the fact that he is not an orphan and lives with his family in Baghdad. Ali's father is an alcoholic and does not work. He also beats Ali's mother and sister regularly. Ali is an exceptionally loving child, full of smiles and always ready to give a hug to everyone around him, but he has few choices in his life.

"Either I have to stay with my mom and sister and protect them when my father comes drunk," Ali told us, "or I have to go in the street, in the traffic, to sell cookies and try to get money."

Amira, a beautiful 15 year old Kurdish girl, has been working in the streets since she was 10. Like Ali, she has a family and home to life in, but she has to work to support her family. "If you saw me sometime, and I am smiling," said Amira, "it's not from bottom of my heart. Inside of me I am very sad because I don't like to go out from my house. But no one works, just me."

Amira's eyes tear up when see sees girls her age that are going to school. She said, "I am in pain because I can't go to school. School is a treasure, and man's future."

Amira refuses to work as a prostitute, but others are not so lucky. Lina is only 14 years old, and already pregnant. [Continued on Page 4]

A child sleeps in one of Baghdad's many alleys-photo by Mohammed Al-Jumah

Al-Muajaha: The Iraqi Witness, Vol. 1, no. 3, 18 June 2003.

·100·

The following three Op-Ed articles were printed in the summer of 2003 in *Al-Muajaha: The Iraqi Witness*, an independent newspaper in Baghdad.

WHO IS RESPONSIBLE?

FREEDOM IS NOT FREEDOM FROM RESPONSIBILITY
Dhiyah Daoud Salman

To whoever will listen to our voices, to whoever can stop our suffering—the tragedy that all Iraqis live in, and more than ever the tragedy of the schools—we will never ask for anything but an end to this suffering.

This is the real message: We teaching staff and students are in distress in so many ways. Who should we look to for solutions? In which direction should we throw our questions?

We were told to return to our schools and to work as we had been working before the war. But when we returned to give what we have to this new station of freedom and all that the word means, throwing away everything of the previous regime, we found:

a) The environmental conditions in the schools are terrible. We have broken windows, crushed doors, and stolen fans, so there is no relief in these hot days.

b) Our curriculum is unresolved. With all the political changes, teachers are not sure, in any official way, what to remove from their lessons or what to add. Without direction, how can they direct their students?

c) No one is broadcasting information in the neighborhoods about the situation in the schools, and so there are many children not attending because their parents are unware; in addition, many parents refuse to let their children go to school because it is generally unsafe everywhere.

There are many points, more than we as teachers could ever list, but our questions begin with: Who is responsible for dealing with these issues? Who will say that this terrible situation is not the fault of the members of this young generation who have only started to cross their way to a new freedom? How will their journey be through all of these difficulties?

Iraq's educators have not received any salaries as of today, and we have families, and they have to live. When we try to press our case with what little administration exists, the answer is: tomorrow, or the next day—or choose any day you wish. Waiting for a salary, how can we perform duties at our best?

We have to ask: Who is responsible? We are without services. With these short words we plead with anyone who is concerned to end this appalling state of affairs.

To teach our students the meaning of freedom in the right way, to teach them all the meanings contained in this word, "freedom," we teachers must look to the future and not stumble toward the past.

Dhiyah Daoud Salman has been a teacher for sixteen years and headmaster of Al-Khawarnaq Primary School in Baghdad for the last three years. He also works as a waiter in order to support his family.

A SENSE OF SECURITY?
My Experience with the Police in the New Iraq
Salaam Talib Al-Onaibi

Last week I was leaving the Palestine Hotel, in the heart of Baghdad, around 9 P.M.—early evening in my old life, but very late in my new one.

The Palestine, a castle surrounded by U.S. troops and barbed wire, is one of the few unquestionably safe places in the city. I hailed a taxi. We hadn't gone far, however, when two men who seemingly needed help signaled for us to stop.

The taxi driver and I behaved like typical Iraqis and welcomed the men with open arms. But after a few moments one of them put a gun in the driver's back, while the other put a knife to my neck. They asked us to empty our pockets, and we did. They stole everything—even the car. Before they drove off, they shot at us, but thank God, no one was hurt.

I had heard that the U.S. military was putting Iraqi police officers back on the street; on TV I saw footage of police on patrol. I didn't think this would solve the city's crime problem, but I thought it was at least a start—I thought there would be someone to protect us.

I could tell you how much money the robbers stole, but that wouldn't help you understand just what this incident really cost me and how much it hurt me: now I feel as if I'm not living in a city, but rather in a jungle of buildings and man-beasts.

I like to stay out late—before the war my friends called me "Night Bat." I would go out after work, and it wasn't until after midnight that my eyes would drift to the clock and I would realize it was time for sleep. During the war, when we all had to go home early—before the worst of the bombing began—I waited impatiently for the day that I could take my old life back.

After the regime fell I could move around the streets again, but the whole city had changed. Buildings were burned out, the streets were full of crushed or stripped-down cars, and everything, even the trees, was covered with dust. Most of all, something was missing inside of me—a sense of security. Every time I saw someone in the street I had to wonder to myself: Is this person a criminal, or someone in need of help?

After I was robbed, I had to know what the police were really doing, who was really responsible for law and order, and whether the U.S. was really trying to restore security, so I started my investigation the next evening at the Palestine Hotel. There are a lot of U.S. forces at the hotel, as well as many Iraqi police; it's just in front of the place—Al-Sadoun Street and Paradise Square—where the TV crews come to film police patrols. Unfortunately, I couldn't find any uniformed policemen there, or anyone else, to make a statement to about what had happened to me the night before.

The hotel staff told me to go to the nearby Al-Alwiyah Club because it had supposedly become a center for U.S. reorganization of the police and Iraqi military forces. I had never been to Al-Alwiyah before—in Saddam's time the Club was only for the privileged.

There were many desks set up inside the Club so that the names of former government workers and policemen could be recorded, but there was no work for them yet. Mohammed Al-Aubaidy, an old police major who waited in the Club hoping to find employment, told me, "This is the third time I've come here, and every time they give me an appointment to come another time. As you see, this is just a useless crowd."

Next I went to the Policemen's College, near Al-Sha'ab Stadium. I entered the building but didn't find anything but walls and empty windows. Everything had been looted. In one of the buildings there was a crowd of people trying to find someone to help them. Four policemen were taking statements from the people, but they weren't able to do anything else to help; they haven't been paid this month, and they aren't sure when their salaries will start again.

The person in charge of registering cases, twenty-four-year-old Officer Omar Lutfy Al-Alosy, told me, "We've got orders to wear civilian dress and stay unarmed. All that we have is a file to write down the name of the complainant and what was stolen."

According to Officer Al-Alosy, they don't have the authority to help anyone, and his superior, General Amer Ali Naif, had ordered some of the police off the streets a few days earlier.

"Of course I don't have the power [to stop criminals], and I can't stop them at all," remarked Officer Al-Alosy.

I then met General Naif, a legal advisor to the appeals court in Baghdad during

In the old Baath Party headquarters in Old Basra, an Iraqi police clerk fills out a report.
LYNSEY ADDARIO/CORBIS 2003

Saddam's time. He corroborated what Officer Al-Alosy had said: "That's right, we received such orders, from General Zuhair Al-Naimi, the police leader, but I think the police force will start working again soon. About the weapons [private militias, such as Ahmed Chalabi's "Free Iraq Fighting Forces," have permission to carry weapons, but the police do not], I think it's hilarious."

I tried to speak with General Zuhair, but his guards wouldn't let me in, so at this point I gave up trying to report my troubles. On May 3 General Zuhair resigned as police chief because he wouldn't run the department in an "American way"; in addition he refused to "enact our laws," according to Captain Jimmy Brownlee, a U.S. Army spokesperson.

Later I heard that some policemen had been arrested in front of the Ministry of Health. A receptionist at the Ministry confirmed that the Americans had arrested two policemen after asking one of them to remove his uniform.

I asked U.S. Major Watkins, in charge of security at the Republican Palace, about the arrested policemen. He told me that the officers arrested may have been abusing their power or simply pretending to be policemen, but people should assume that anyone dressed as a police officer is, in fact, legitimate.

I went to the police station in Huriya. The station was hit with cluster bombs during the war and then looted afterwards. While I was there a U.S. military officer came to the station and put up a sign in English that read, "Police." According to the Iraqi policemen there, the U.S. asked them, "Who gave you permission to be here?"

Perhaps that question should be asked in reverse—by the policemen of the Americans.

_____

Salaam Talib Al-Onaibi is a twenty-eight-year-old computer engineer in Baghdad.

WHO IS RESPONSIBLE?
Hamsa Mohammed

In our daily lives, are we seeing and reading the truth? We have to dive beneath the surface appearances that are presented to us.

When the American and British armies entered Iraq, they called themselves liberators. They said they came to liberate Iraqis from an oppressive, murderous government, and to prevent the spread of weapons of mass destruction. Did these "liberators" cross all the continents to arrive in Iraq simply for the safety of the Iraqi people? Who will cover the costs of these noble volunteers?

And while we are on the subject: May I ask where, exactly, Saddam and his world-threatening weapons are today?

I want facts. After thirteen years of an embargo that prevented anything from entering Iraq without United Nations authorization, no one has found any weapons of mass destruction. After eight years of weapons inspections using the most modern techniques (from 1991 to 1998), no one has found any weapons of mass destruction. In these last months of renewed international inspections and renewed Anglo-American war-making, no one has found any weapons of mass destruction. Can we conclude that the fact is that there are no weapons of mass destruction? Or maybe Saddam is storing them in the White House beneath Bush's bed?

Saddam Hussein was not Iraq. It doesn't make sense to punish twenty-four million people—to make them suffer hunger, illness, and death—because of one person and his imaginary weapons. It is illegal and inhumane to murder an entire nation based on suspicions. Who is responsible for all the deaths caused by the sanctions?

If suspicions were enough to punish Iraq, then when is the very real evidence of Israel's weapons of mass destruction going to be enough to punish Israel? Justice should be evenly applied. Anything else is the judgment of the strong on the weak. It is the law of the jungle.

The end of both Saddam and the sanctions is a dream that most Iraqis have been eagerly awaiting. Iraq is rich with its fortunes, and rich with a civilization that dates back thousands of years. We can rebuild our country by ourselves. But now we have a new Saddam—the Americans. And now we have a new sanctions regime—the Americans have put their hands on every piece of paper that leads to every single drop of Iraq's oil. We still cannot control our own future.

They say they are here to bring freedom back to Iraqis, but the first hands we see are the hands of Paul Bremer and Jay Garner, our new rulers, and Philip Carroll, appointed as the man responsible for Iraqi oil. I'm just wondering: Is "Philip Carroll" an Iraqi name?

Who is responsible for these appointments? And who is responsible for the distribution of all the contracts to American companies for "rebuilding" Iraq? Are Iraqis responsible? Or Americans? Or Americans wearing Iraqi clothes (such as Ahmed Chalabi)?

The American soldiers say their task is to keep us safe and provide security for civilians, but the looting and other crimes continue to this day. And what about the massacres in Mosul and Falluja and elsewhere? Dozens have been killed. What about the Al-Zafarania accident, where at least nine innocent people lost their lives? What about the "controlled explosions" of weapons the Americans are conducting all over town, which frighten people every day? Are these explosions really controlled? Go to the Adhamia and judge for yourselves—three houses were destroyed because of such explosions, and many people were wounded.

Who is responsible? Who will take responsibility for these disasters?

What Iraq needs now is a government representative of Iraqis—not Americans—which will organize and maintain security, and take responsibility for all that Iraq suffers from.

Hamsa Mohammed is a twenty-two-year-old Iraqi college student at Baghdad University where she is captain of the women's volleyball team. She hopes to be a writer.

BAGHDAD JOURNAL #6

I have a meeting at the United Nations Development Program (UNDP). The UNDP is about a mile from the Andaluz Apartments, where I am staying. This is the first time that I've been out on my own—and we've been told over and over again not to go out alone, but no one is available to come with me, and I have an appointment to keep. I've decided to walk because I've heard that cabs aren't always safe for women traveling alone.

I walk along the Tigris in the heat and the dust, my heart pounding in my ears. About halfway there, a tank blocks the street. For blocks I walk straight towards a huge cannon, seemingly aimed at me.

Hundreds of Iraqis are lined up behind the tank, waiting in front of a metal gate guarded by GIs. They are communications workers who haven't been paid for weeks. They are still waiting when I return an hour later.

I walk past boarded-up, bombed-out buildings. One building is in the process of reconstruction; an Iraqi man and his sons are working away, and it looks as if they've almost completed the job. Why is it that they can make so much progress, I wonder, when so much of the rest of Baghdad remains a war zone? Why hasn't the CPA, with all the power of the United States behind it, done more to improve conditions here? An occupier is responsible for the conditions in the place it occupies: it is responsible for security, for essential services, for people's health and safety. This place is not safe.

A man, obviously drunk, stumbles towards me, grabs me, and tries to steal my purse. For some reason, I stay calm; he seems harmless. Other men come down the street to rescue me. They reprimand him and tell him to leave me alone. Afterwards, they apologize for his behavior.

In February, seeing someone intoxicated here was a rarity. On this walk I see about fifteen men who are obviously drunk. Street kids are everywhere, and I pass a huddle of them sniffing glue.

The streets are empty of women.

As I continue to walk, I hear repeated and frequent catcalls from the passing taxis. This is also new. The men seem drunk or high on something—perhaps just on their sudden freedom.

The UNDP buildings have been totally bombed-out and looted, the back buildings have been rebuilt, and new furnishing and equipment have been installed—another example of a reconstruction not involving the CPA. My contact at the UNDP, Omar, tells me it was all done with Iraqi labor.

"Who is actually confronting their fear and who is running from it?" he asks as we sit together. "Iraqis are afraid of civil war—it is how Saddam kept us under his control, the threat that without him we would kill each other." Omar is very serious and concerned; this is very difficult for him and the solution is not clear. "The mistake has already been made," he says. He is upset about the talk that a constitution is being written by some student in his twenties in a university in New York. "It is rather absurd and another expression of disrespect. The constitution needs to flow from our culture and our religion. I don't believe in the civil war fear anymore; together we can do better than what we are living with now. Iraqis need to rebuild their lives and their country."

Omar talks about all the friends and relatives he knows who are in custody at the airport and the anger that is felt in the neighborhoods. He calls over his colleagues, and each has a story about someone they know being taken away in the night with no word on their whereabouts or their condition. Even with their official positions at UNDP, they have no access or information.

After my meeting at the UNDP I walk to the Palestine Hotel, which is close to the Andaluz Apartments. I want to find Terry, who works for a nongovernmental agency funded by the United States Agency for International Development (USAID). We had met the night before at the hotel; Terry had stories about

and sewage spilled in the streets, and I wanted to know more.

I am drenched with sweat from fear and heat. This is an area where we hear gunfire every night, and I know that it's not safe even now.

GIs guard the entrances to the two big hotels where foreigners stay; they frisk me and ask me for ID as they stand by their Humvees in the blazing heat, and street kids cluster around. One of the soldiers tells me how he washed the hair of a cute little girl yesterday, and I am both touched and concerned—I think of the kids, so dirty and uncared for, and the soldiers, standing here all day with no shade, so vulnerable despite their body armor and gear, verifying the IDs of the occasional pedestrian and checking the GMCs that barrel through the checkpoints to the hotels.

As I approach the lobby of the Palestine, vendors hawk newspapers.

Private First Class Christopher Pusateri of the 82nd Airborne Division passes his sunglasses around to a group of Iraqi kids while patrolling in Baghdad. LYNSEY ADDARIO/CORBIS 2003

Baghdad neighborhoods with no water. One is in Arabic and English: "Baghdad

Now, A Bi-weekly First Armored Division Publication." Inside are articles about the new Iraqi police force, about the need for good sanitary practices ("A Partnership to Remove Trash"), and most interesting to me, "The Coalition Mission." "The United States and its Coalition partners are dedicated to returning Iraq to the Iraqi people as soon as possible," the article states. "However, they stand by their pledge to ensure a safe and stable country before withdrawing its troops."

The article goes on to talk about "Operation Neighborhood"—"one of the many programs underway to help the Iraqi people rebuild their communities and country. Rebuilding neighborhoods is one of the first steps toward rebuilding Iraq." It promises that newly formed neighborhood councils, the CPA, the U.S. military, and its coalition part-

ners "are working to eliminate those who would stand in the way of a new Iraq—Ba'athists, Fadayeen, and criminals. There will be more soldiers and police officers on the streets preventing crime and apprehending criminals. Iraqis can also help create a safe and stable community by turning in large-caliber weapons. . . . In a modern, free society the majority of Iraq citizens have no need to carry weapons."

I am thinking about sending this article to the NRA.

Continued . . .

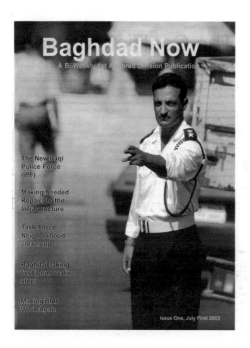

Baghdad Now: A Bi-weekly 1st Armored Division Publication, Issue One, 1 July 2003.

The Coalition Mission

The United States and its Coalition partners are dedicated to returning Iraq to the Iraqi people as soon as possible.

However, they stand by their pledge to ensure a safe and stable country before withdrawing its troops.

Several programs are underway to help the Iraqi people rebuild their country. Soldiers and staff of the Office of the Coalition Provisional Authority are working together in Iraq's communities to rebuild its infrastructure, provide a safe and secure environment and promote self-government.

Military engineers have been going into neighborhoods in Baghdad and other cities to help citizens rebuild their communities. Operation Neighborhood is a program that teams engineers with members of the community in its rebuilding projects.

Recently, soldiers from the 1st Armored Division went to the Abu Ghurayb neighborhood rebuild their community marketplace June 5.

Engineers from the 94th Engineer Battalion repaired the local primary school and cleared tons of rubbish from the streets. They helped reestablish the local economy by building and setting 30 market stalls. They also improved the area's recreation facilities by smoothing the local soccer field.

Operation Neighborhood is one of many programs underway to help the Iraqi people rebuild their communities and country. Rebuilding neighborhoods is one of the first steps toward rebuilding Iraq.

In addition to making needed repairs, Operation Neighborhood provides jobs to residents.

On a larger scale, engineers are working to rebuild the city's waters, electric, sewage and roadways.

Throughout the city of Baghdad, residents are joining together to form local neighborhood advisory councils. These councils will form the foundation of a new government for the Iraqi people – one that represents their needs and responds to their communities.

The United States and its Coalition partners are dedicated to returning Iraq to the Iraqi people as soon as possible.

City residents are forming their neighborhood councils in each of the city's 90 district neighborhoods.

The neighborhood councils will elect district councils over the next several weeks. The election of the district councils is the second step leading to the formation of the Baghdad City Council on June 30th.

The neighborhood councils give the people of Baghdad a voice in their own government and a forum for citizens to address their concerns

Neighborhood councils will have many resources at their disposal to solve problems. It can also seek assistance from the district or city-wide council.

Councils work directly with military commanders and representatives of the Office of the Coalition Provisional Authority to solve problems in their neighborhoods.

Backing up those councils will be a trained and professional police force.

OCPA, the U.S. military, its coalition partners and members of the community are working to eliminate those who would stand in the way a new Iraq – Ba'athists, Fadayeen, and criminals.

There will be more soldiers and police officers on the streets preventing crime and apprehending criminals.

Soldiers will seek out and apprehend members of the former regime, terrorists and members of the Iraqi military who have not surrendered or continue to fight against Coalition Forces.

Iraqis can also help create a safe and stable community by turning in large-caliber weapons.

The intent of the heavy weapons turn-in program is not to disarm the Iraqi people but one of many programs designed to promote a safe and secure communities

All members of the community are encouraged to participate in this effort. Those who do not possess large-caliber weapons are encouraged to get those who do to turn over their weapons, show weapons caches to authorities and to report illegal weapons sellers to authorities.

In a modern, free society the majority of Iraq citizens have no need to carry weapons. By working with the newly formed government and police force, taking part in community rebuilding efforts and helping fight crime on their communist, the Iraqi people can hasten the day when Coalition Forces leave their country.

Baghdad

"Coalition Mission," *Baghdad Now: A Bi-weekly 1st Armored Division Publication*, Issue One, 1 July 2003.

BAGHDAD JOURNAL #6

At a propane distribution, thousands of Iraqi civilians clamor for aid, as American soldiers from the First Cavalry Division take down an Iraqi civilian. LYNSEY ADDARIO/CORBIS 2003

STRETCHED THIN, LIED TO, AND MISTREATED

ON THE GROUND WITH U.S. TROOPS IN IRAQ

An M-16 rifle hangs by a cramped military cot. On the wall above is a message in thick black ink: "Ali Baba, you owe me a strawberry milk!"

It's a private joke but could just as easily summarize the worldview of American soldiers here in Baghdad, the fetid basement of Donald Rumsfeld's house of victory. Trapped in the polluted heat, poorly supplied, and cut off from regular news, the GIs are fighting a guerrilla war that they neither wanted, expected, nor trained for. On the urban battlefields of central Iraq, "shock and awe" and all the other "new way of war" buzzwords are drowned out by the din of diesel-powered generators, Islamic prayer calls, and the occasional pop of small-arms fire.

Here, the high-tech weaponry that so emboldens Pentagon bureaucrats is largely useless, and the grinding work of counterinsurgency is done the old-fashioned way— by hand. Not surprisingly, most of the American GIs stuck with the job are weary, frustrated, and ready to go home.

It is noon and the mercury is hanging steady at 115 degrees Fahrenheit. The filmmaker Garrett Scott and I are "embedded" with Alpha Company of the Third Battalion of the 124th Infantry, a Florida National Guard unit about half of whom did time in the regular Army, often with elite groups like the Rangers. Like most frontline troops in Iraq, the majority are white, but there is a sizable minority of African-American and Latino soldiers among them. Unlike most combat units, about 65 percent are college students—they've traded six years with the Guard for tuition at Florida State. Typically, that means occasional weekends in the Everglades or directing traffic during hurricanes. Instead, these guys got sent to Iraq, and as yet they have no sure departure date.

Mobilized in December, they crossed over from Kuwait on day one of the invasion and are now bivouacked in the looted remains of a Republican Guard officers' club, a modernist slab of polished marble and tinted glass that the GIs have fortified with plywood, sandbags, and razor wire.

Behind "the club" is a three-story dormitory, a warren of small one-bedroom apartments, each holding a nine-man squad of soldiers and all their gear. Around two hundred guys are packed in here. Their sweaty fatigues drape the banisters of the exterior stairway, while inside the cramped, dark rooms the floors are covered with cots, heaps of flak vests, guns, and, where possible, big tin, water-based air-conditioners called swamp coolers. Surrounding the base is a chaotic working-class neighborhood of two- and three-story cement homes and apartment buildings. Not far away is the muddy Tigris River.

This company limits patrols to three or four hours a day. For the many hours in between, the guys pull guard duty, hang out in their cavelike rooms, or work out in a makeshift weight room.

"We're getting just a little bit stir-crazy," explains lanky Sergeant Sellers. His demeanor is typical of the nine-man squad we have been assigned to, friendly but serious, with a wry and angry sense of humor. On the side of his helmet Sellers has, in violation of regs, attached the unmistakable pin and ring of a hand grenade. Next to it is written, "Pull Here."

Leaning back on a cot, he's drawing a large, intricate pattern on a female mannequin leg. The wall above him displays a photocollage of pictures retrieved from a looted Iraqi women's college. Smiling young ladies wearing the *hijab* sip sodas and stroll past buses. They seem to be on some sort of field trip. Nearby are photos clipped from *Maxim* of coy young American girls offering up their pert round bottoms. Dominating it all is a large hand-drawn dragon and a photo of Jessica Lynch with a bubble caption reading: "Hi, I am a war hero. And I think that weapons maintenance is totally unimportant."

The boys don't like Lynch and find the story of her rescue ridiculous. They'd been down the same road a day earlier and are unsympathetic. "We just feel that it's unfair and kind of distorted the way the whole Jessica, quote, 'rescue' thing got hyped," explains Staff Sergeant Kreed Howell. He is in charge of the squad, and at thirty-one a bit older than most of his men. Muscular and clean-cut, Howell is a relaxed and natural leader, with the gracious bearing of a proper Southern upbringing.

"In other words, you'd have to be really fucking dumb to get lost on the road," says another, less diplomatic soldier.

Specialist John Crawford sits in a tiny, windowless supply closet that is loaded with packs and gear. He is two credits short of a BA in anthropology and wants to go to graduate school. Howell, a Republican, amicably describes Crawford as the squad's house liberal.

There's just enough extra room in the closet for Crawford, a chair, and a little shelf on which sits a laptop. Hanging by this makeshift desk is a handwritten sign from "the management" requesting that soldiers masturbating in the supply closet "remove their donations in a receptacle." Instead of watching pornography DVDs, Crawford is here to finish a short story. "Trying to start writing again," he says.

Crawford is a fan of Tim O'Brien, particularly *The Things They Carried*. We chat, then he shows me his short story. It's about a vet who is back home in north Florida trying to deal with the memory of having accidentally blown away a child while serving in Iraq.

Later, in the cramped main room, Sellers and Sergeant Brunelle, another one of the squad's more gregarious and dominant personalities, are matter-of-factly showing us digital photos of dead Iraqis.

"These guys shot at some of our guys, so we lit 'em up. Put two .50-cal rounds in their vehicle. One went through this dude's hip and into the other guy's head," explains Brunelle. The third man in the car lived. "His buddy was crying like a baby. Just sitting there bawling with his friend's brains and skull fragments all over his face. One of our guys came up to him and is like: 'Hey! No crying in baseball!'"

"I know that probably sounds sick," says Sellers, "but humor is the only way you can deal with this shit."

And just below the humor is volcanic rage. These guys are proud to be soldiers and don't want to come across as whiners, but they are furious about what they've been through. They hate having their lives disrupted and put at risk. They hate the military for its stupidity, its feckless lieutenants and blowhard brass living comfortably in Saddam's palaces. They hate Iraqis—or, as they say, *"hajis"*—for trying to kill them. They hate the country for its dust, heat, and sewage-clogged streets. They hate having killed people. Some even hate the politics of the war. And because most of them are, ultimately, just regular well-intentioned guys, one senses the distinct fear that someday a few may hate themselves for what they have been forced to do here.

Added to such injury is insult: The military treats these soldiers like unwanted stepchildren. This unit's rifles are retooled hand-me-downs from Vietnam. They have inadequate radio gear, so they buy their own unencrypted Motorola walkie-talkies. The same goes for flashlights, knives, and some components for night-vision sights.

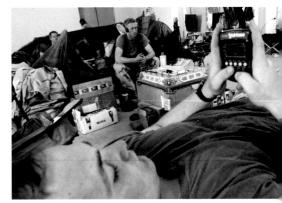

The low-performance Iraqi air-conditioners and fans, as well as the one satellite phone and payment cards shared by the whole company for calling home, were also purchased out of pocket from civilian suppliers.

Bottled water rations are kept to two liters a day. After that the guys drink from "water buffaloes"—big, hot, chlorination tanks that turn the amoeba-infested dreck from the local taps into something like swimming-pool water. Mix this with powdered Gatorade and you can wash down afamously bad MRE (Meal, Ready-to-Eat).

To top it all off they must endure the pathologically uptight culture of the Army hierarchy. The Third of the 124th is now

Specialist Eric Martin, 24, of Ricetown, Wisconsin, with the 3rd Infantry Division, 2nd Brigade, listens to music as Private First Class David Brock plays video games. LYNSEY ADDARIO/CORBIS 2003

attached to the newly arrived First Armored Division, and when it is time to raid suspected resistance cells it's the Guardsmen who have to kick in the doors and clear the apartments.

"The First AD wants us to catch bullets for them but won't give us enough water, doesn't let us wear do-rags, and makes us roll down our shirtsleeves so we look proper! Can you believe that shit?" Sergeant Sellers is pissed off.

The soldiers' improvisation extends to food as well. After a month or so of occupying "the club," the company commander, Captain Sanchez, allowed two Iraqi entrepreneurs to open shop on his side of the wire—one runs a slow Internet cafe, the other a kebab stand where the "Joes" pay U.S. dollars for grilled lamb on flatbread.

"The *haji* stand is one of the only things we have to look forward to, but the First AD keeps getting scared and shutting it down." Sellers is on a roll, but he's not alone.

Even the lighthearted Howell, who insists that the squad has it better than most troops, chimes in. "The one thing I will say is that we have been here entirely too long. If I am not home by Christmas my business will fail." Back "on earth" (in Panama City, Florida), Howell is a building contractor with a wife, two small children, equipment, debts, and employees.

Perhaps the most shocking bit of military incompetence is the unit's lack of formal training in what's called "close-quarter combat." The urbanized mayhem of Mogadishu may loom large in the discourse of the military's academic journals like *Parameters* and the *Naval War College Review*, but many U.S. infantrymen are trained only in large-scale, open-country maneuvers—how to defend Germany from

a wave of Russian tanks.

So, since "the end of the war" these guys have had to retrain themselves in the dark arts of urban combat. "The houses here are small, too," says Brunelle. "Once you're inside you can barely get your rifle up. You got women screaming, people, furniture everywhere. It's insane."

By now this company has conducted scores of raids, taken fire on the street, taken casualties, taken rocket-propelled grenade attacks to "the club," and are defiantly proud of the fact that they have essentially been abandoned, survived, retrained themselves, and can keep a lid on their little piece of Baghdad. But it's not always the Joes who have the upper hand. Increasingly, Haji seems to set the agenda.

A thick black plume of smoke rises from Karrada Street, a popular electronics district where U.S. patrols often buy air-conditioners and DVDs. An American Humvee, making just such a stop, has been blown to pieces by a remote-activated "improvised explosive device," or IED, buried in the median between two lanes of traffic. By chance two colleagues and I are the first press on the scene. The street is empty of traffic and quiet except for the local shopkeepers, who occasionally call out to us in Arabic and English: "Be careful."

Finally we get close enough to see clearly. About twenty feet away is a military transport truck and a Humvee, and beyond that are the flaming remains of a third Humvee. A handful of American soldiers are crouched behind the truck, totally still. There's no firing, no yelling, no talking, no radio traffic. No one is screaming, but two GIs are down. As yet there are no reinforcements or helicopters overhead. All one can hear is the burning of the Humvee.

Then it begins: The ammunition in the burning Humvee starts to explode, and the troops in the street start firing. Armored personnel carriers arrive and disgorge dozens of soldiers from the 82nd Airborne to join the fight. The target is a three-story office building just across from the engulfed Humvee. Occasionally we hear a few rounds of return fire pass by like hot razors slashing straight lines through the air. The really close rounds just sound like loud cracks.

"That's Kalashnikov. I know the voice," says Ahmed, our friend and translator. There is a distinct note of national pride in his voice—his countrymen are fighting back—never mind the fact that we are now mixed in with the most forward U.S. troops and getting shot at.

The firefight goes on for about two hours, moving slowly and methodically. It is in many ways an encapsulation of the whole war—confusing and labor-intensive. The GIs have more firepower than they can use, and they don't even know exactly where or who the enemy is. Civilians are hiding in every corner, the ground floor of the target building is full of merchants and shoppers, and undisciplined fire could mean scores of dead civilians.

There are two GIs on the ground, one with his legs gone and probably set to die. When a medevac helicopter arrives just overhead, it, too, like much other technology, is foiled. The street is crisscrossed with electrical wires and there is no way the chopper can land to extract the wounded. The soldiers around us look grave and tired.

Eventually some Bradley fighting vehicles start pounding the building with mean 250-millimeter cannon shells. Whoever might have been shooting from upstairs is either dead or gone.

The street is now littered with overturned air-conditioners, fans, and refrigerators. A cooler of sodas sits forlorn on the sidewalk. Farther away two civilians lie dead, caught in the crossfire. A soldier peeks out from the hatch of a Bradley and calls over to a journalist, "Hey, can you grab me one of those Cokes?"

After the shootout we promised ourselves we'd stay out of Humvees and away from U.S. soldiers. But that was yesterday. Now Crawford is helping us put on body armor, and soon we'll be on patrol. As we move out with the nine soldiers the mood is somewhere between tense and bored. Crawford mockingly introduces himself to no one in particular: "John Crawford, I work in population reduction."

"Watch the garbage—if you see wires coming out of a pile it's an IED," warns Howell. The patrol is uneventful. We walk fast through back streets and rubbish-strewn lots, pouring sweat in the late afternoon heat. Local residents watch the small squad with a mixture of civility, indifference, and open hostility. An Iraqi man shouts, "When? When? When? Go!" The soldiers ignore him.

"Sometimes we sham," explains one of the guys. "We'll just go out and kick it behind some wall. Watch what's going on but skip the walking. And sometimes at night we get sneaky-deaky. Creep up on Haji, so he knows we're all around."

"I am just walking to be walking," says the laconic Fredrick Pearson, aka "Diddy," the only African-American in Howell's squad. Back home he works in the State Supreme Court bureaucracy and plans to go to law school. "I just keep an eye on the rooftops, look around, and walk."

The patrols aren't always peaceful. One soldier mentions that he recently "kicked the shit out of a twelve-year-old kid" who menaced him with a toy gun.

Later we roll with the squad on another patrol, this time at night and in two Humvees. Now there's more evident hostility from the young Iraqi men loitering in the dark. Most of these infantry soldiers don't like being stuck in vehicles. At a blacked-out corner where a particularly large group of youths is clustered, the Humvees stop and Howell bails out into the crowd. There is no interpreter along tonight.

"Hey, guys! What's up? How y'all doing? OK? Everything OK? All right?" asks Howell in his jaunty, laid-back, north Florida accent. The sullen young men fade away into the dark, except for two, who shake the sergeant's hand. Howell's attempt to take the high road, winning hearts and minds, doesn't seem to be for show. He really believes in this war. But in the torrid gloom of the Baghdad night, his efforts seem tragically doomed.

Watching Howell I think about the civilian technocrats working with Paul Bremer at the Coalition Provisional Authority; the electricity is out half the time, and these folks hold meetings on how best to privatize state industries and end food rations. Meanwhile, the city seethes. The Pentagon, likewise, seems to have no clear plan; its troops are stretched thin, lied to, and mistreated. The whole charade feels increasingly patched together, poorly improvised. Ultimately, there's very little that Howell and his squad can do about any of this. After all, it's not their war. They just work here.

PREVIOUS SPREAD: U.S. troops patrol the streets while convoying through Baghdad. LYNSEY ADDARIO/CORBIS 2003

RESISTING EMPIRE:
LESSONS FOR IRAQ FROM PALESTINE

As I sit here, not far from the Muqata'a, Yasir Arafat's besieged and mostly destroyed office, I wonder how the Iraqi people are ever going to rid themselves of their occupation. Nothing Palestinians have done in the last decade of so-called "peacemaking" has managed to extricate them from their occupation. Indeed, looking back there was little chance the peace process would lead to peace; like Palestinians, Iraqis don't have the luxury of a wasted decade before they take matters into their own hands.

Listening to the shouts of schoolchildren pledging loyalty to their erstwhile leader, I can't help wonder what lessons this occupation has for Iraqis struggling against Israel's chief benefactor. Palestinians have tried seemingly everything: armed guerilla struggle, popular insurrection, terrorism, negotiations, mass nonviolent civil protests. Yet Israel, like the "house" in a Vegas casino, always wins in the end—this despite the fact that its ever intensifying occupation is reaching a level of brutality and dehumanization that is shocking in its banality as much as its scope.

Palestinians continue to put their faith in symbolic leaders like Arafat, yet these leaders almost always are corrupted and in the end will fail their people when integrity, honesty, brains, and courage are needed most. It's not surprising that the political leadership of the increasingly irrelevant Palestinian Authority (PA) are almost entirely middle-aged or older men with histories of corruption and accommodation with power—Israel has eliminated or exiled anyone with better credentials. At the same time, however, one of the main reasons that Arafat is still personally so important for Palestinians is that however inept and venal his rule, he ultimately has refused completely to sell out Palestinian national independence. As one Palestinian friend put it, "He's a dictator, but a nationalist one," and this dynamic, especially for a nation under such threat to its existence, is what has helped him remain a central figure, even as Palestinians increasingly consider him irrelevant on a day-to-day basis of struggle and survival.

The Iraqis chosen by the U.S. to lead their country to supposed independence appear little better than their counterparts in the PA, and in fact, the plan to privatize and sell off to foreign interests literally the entire Iraqi economy save for the oil industry (where we can assume the U.S. has already secured sweetheart deals with its protégés in the Oil Ministry) reveals the extent of the corruption shared between the occupier and the occupied elite. The pattern for such a sell-off of the national economy—if not national independence per se—follows the same path as most other processes of "independence" where the "mother" country retained preferential positions in crucial economic sectors. In Palestine the 1994 Paris Protocols went so far as to prevent "either side" from developing any new industry that could compete with an existing industry of the other. Needless to say, with Israel having one of the most advanced economies on earth and Palestine reeling from three decades of occupation,

Palestinian leaders wound up signing away the rights to develop almost any new industry save boutique flowers and other specialized agricultural production—much of which is held up and allowed to rot at checkpoints whenever Israel wants to send a message. Let's not forget that both these economic plans were sold under the aura of a "New Middle East" built on the foundations of democracy and free markets; Iraqis can look to Palestine if they want to know where that fantasy leads.

As I talk with the young generation of emerging Palestinian grass roots leaders—well-educated twenty- and thirty-somethings from a variety of class and social backgrounds—I realize that if there is hope for Iraqis and Palestinians alike, it is going to come from truly radical young people who are committed both to comprehensive social transformation and to resistance, but in a manner that moves beyond the kind of crude nationalism, ethnic exclusivism, or violence that has proved so morally and politically counterproductive. Only such a positive culture of resistance can hope to defeat the full weight of colonialism and occupation in the global age. Yet in Palestine too many of this generation are already being co-opted and depoliticized by a surprising source: the international nongovernmental organization (NGO) community whose "civil society" and related "capacity building" programs have, ironically, created a Palestinian intellectual and activist/NGO class whose disconnection from the needs and realities of the grassroots—as well as the intensification of occupation—increases in direct proportion to its funding.

As the well-intentioned world NGO community rushes in to save Iraq from America, it would do well to take stock of the reasons behind the failures of the NGO/civil society system in Palestine. One the one hand, it is clear that positively radical social movements and forces such as are desperately needed in Palestine or Iraq absolutely need international support. Yet it is precisely because of who the main providers of that support have been in Palestine—and are as of now in Iraq—that such problems have occurred: that is, the main groups delivering a message of human freedom, democracy, and development have wound up being associated with policies that have been disastrous for people on the ground. In Palestine it's been an NGO community that hasn't been able to tackle the root causes of occupation or focus successfully on society-wide grassroots activities and whose relatively large sums of money poured into a relatively small intellectual class have tended to weaken rather than strengthen that class's bond with the rest of society. In Iraq, of course, the UN has become the tragic example of this problem, as it offered itself as the provider of humanitarian relief and even a political counterpoint to the U.S. occupation regime when in fact it was implicated in ten years of devastating sanctions and then rubber-stamped the invasion itself; these policies have made it difficult to be seen as neutral or even sympathetic to the needs of ordinary Iraqis.

The violence that shattered the UN presence has also played a crucial role in Palestine, where a major reason for the depoliticization of the NGO class has been the violence of the Israeli occupation. In fact, both Palestine and Iraq are the product of extreme violence associated with uncompromising colonialism. In his essay in this book, Mike Davis details the legacy of British rule in Iraq; the violence of 1920 profoundly impacted the dynamics of politics to this day. Like Israel's occupation of Palestine, Britain's occupation of Iraq could only be implemented by extreme violence and autocratic rule, including the repeated use of poison gas and large-scale aerial bombings of civilian targets which have made Saddam Hussein infamous, and which, according to a recent biography of Hussein, "administered a shock to the country's social system from which it has never recovered. It was the British conquest of Iraq which set the stage for what is happening today."

Violence has had a similarly profound impact on Palestinian society (and Israeli society as well, with lessons that all Americans should heed if they don't want to wind up living in a society as hypermilitarized and uncivil as Israel's). For Iraqis the biggest lesson is the disempowering effect of overwhelming violence: the victims of the violence are unable to transcend it in order to develop large-scale societal means of resistance that don't mirror the same violence and associated pathologies.

For example, in conversations with numerous Palestinian leaders, including

Sergeant Valdez with the 1st Armored Division fires shots into the air to try to control the crowd.
LYNSEY ADDARIO/CORBIS 2003

leaders of Hamas, most accept that the violence used by militant Palestinian groups against Israeli civilians is not achieving any concrete political goals, is counterproductive, and is playing right into Ariel Sharon's hands. However, many also feel either that they have had to engage in such violence so that Israelis would at least feel some of the Palestinian's pain and suffering, or that there was no realistic alternative available to surrender or personally/politically suicidal violence. In other words, the cycle of violence has so stifled Palestinian creative political energies that only a small but crucial segment of society can resist responding with their own extreme violence. This is destroying any chance for independence, not to mention a viable social fabric within which to continue resistance.

In this context the most important issue for Iraqis to learn from Palestine is the need to confront dehumanization: the occupation of Palestine continues to succeed because successive Israeli governments have engaged in dehumanizing Palestinians to such a degree that just living one's daily life has become a supreme but largely unacknowledged act of nonviolent resistance. This societal *summud* (steadfastness)—the result of the combination of brutality and indoctrination within Israeli society, where, for example, newly conscripted Israeli soldiers are told that Arabs are animals and every Palestinian wants to kill every Jew possible—has produced a level of psychosis within Israeli culture, which in turn has tended to create a vicious cycle where Palestinians internalize the hatred of Israelis and reply in kind. This damages the positive aspect and process of *summud* that is at the core of Palestinian identity and survival.

Everything possible must be done to prevent a similar process from occurring in Iraq: simplification and demonizing of the U.S. and the West are already at the heart of the discourse of Al-Qaeda. The U.S. is already exploiting this dynamic: in fact, their goal seems to be to sow enough chaos and violence so that Iraqi society breaks down and is left with little ability to develop any creative and politically effective means of resistance.

Given the similarly violent conditions in Palestine and Iraq, what strategies can be adopted in Iraq based on the lessons of Palestine? A lot of work remains to be done to answer this question, but here are a few of the things Palestine teaches us:

1. The occupation of Palestine has succeeded in good measure because Israel has been able to play off and accentuate class and ethnic differences within Palestinian society through political and economic control. The destruction of Palestinian civil society has made it much easier for violence to become the main form of resistance. Every effort must be made to help Iraqis build a grassroots democratic society and to ensure that the U.S. doesn't succeed in dividing the country along ethnic lines.

2. The International Solidarity Movement (ISM) remains perhaps the most important model for Iraq, and for it to work Iraqis must take the lead. What is needed in Iraq, specifically, is an ISM-type force that clearly distinguishes itself from the U.S. and the UN/mainstream NGO community so that its message cannot be implicated in the larger dynamics of the occupation. At the same time, strategically, it should develop through a two-stage process: first, by forming the nucleus of an international force that protects Iraqis from the vagaries of U.S. occupation by monitoring what the U.S. is doing and that does what the U.S. fails to do (as Occupation Watch is already doing). Then, after local legitimacy is built through these kinds of activities, a kind of ISM "Peace Corps" of volunteer doctors, lawyers, agriculturalists, and similar crucial professions must be developed which can forge links with progressive local forces. This would allow not just resistance to the occupation, but the building of an alternative social fabric on the ground with strong links to the global peace and justice movement.

3. Americans must become educated. One of the main reasons Palestine gets so little sympathy from Americans is that our view of the history of the Israeli-Palestinian conflict is so distorted and inaccurate. Having recently looked at the textbooks used for teaching California students about Iraq, it is clear to me that our government and its corporate media allies—the materials are all produced by large media companies—are similarly trying to prevent any understanding of the realities of British colonial rule in Iraq or American foreign policy towards Iraq. Most Americans remain ignorant of our unflinching support for "the dictator Saddam

Hussein" (which included putting his Baath party in power twice, in 1963 and 1968, and helping to find and kill thousands of Iraqi communists in the process), just as we have been inoculated against the real history of our involvement with coups and corrupt dictatorial regimes in every other country in the region.

An effort must be made to look at the history of the region systematically and holistically, to help Americans understand the links between our support for Israel and for Saudi Arabia, the power of the "arms-petrodollar cycle," and the coalition of big oil and defense companies which has benefited for decades to the tune of upwards of 13 percent of the profits of the Fortune 500. With the invasion and occupation of Iraq, this coalition has managed to succeed in the greatest theft in history of American tax dollars and another country's resources.

4. Needless to say, the military-industrial complex behind the current occupation is intimately related to the processes of globalization. It's not for nothing that the World Bank, that paragon of neoliberal market mythology, argued almost a decade ago that in order to create the "new social contract" necessary to bring the Middle East into the global age, civil societies will have to "lower their protective walls" while governments lower wages and subsidies in the name of efficiency and productivity, all of which was likely to necessitate a "shakedown period to clear out the accumulated structural problems" of the region.

George W. Bush and Co. clearly felt a shakedown was not sufficient; instead, "shock and awe" were necessary to free Iraq from the shackles of a history that, as the Arab economist Samir Amin long ago pointed out, has been tied into the world capitalist system longer than other region of the Third World aside from Latin America—specifically, as a marginalized and peripheral region whose main resource, oil, has become the main obstacle to autonomous and democratic development.

5. Our artists, academics, and activists must grapple with the increasingly clear fact that the occupations of Iraq and Palestine represent (like Stalinism, the Holocaust, slavery, and the genocide of indigenous Americans, etc.) the absolute failure of what the Moroccan Islamist activist and Sufi leader Abdesalam Yassine calls "armed capitalist modernity." (Yassine's phrase echoes the description posited by the socialist philosopher George Sorel a century ago of the inherent similarity between "the capitalist type and the warrior type.")

We need to create an entirely new philosophy, ethics, and aesthetics—that is, a truly new social contract—to enable humanity to imagine and work towards a better future. But in order to do that we need to be asking the right questions and demanding honest answers of ourselves as much as of those in power. From this perspective, Palestine sends a message to the Iraqi people: Be smart, don't waste one or two generations with fantasies, corrupt leaders, and illusions of peace. Do the hard work now and build social movements to bring justice and democracy from the grassroots.

More broadly, as Sheikh Yassine points out, we need to "address modernity with questions it has no interest in, and which its citizens haven't the time to ask . . ." The dialogue of the deaf leading up to the Iraqi invasion clearly demonstrates that "two-way communication is beyond reach with a modernity that is comfortably installed in a way of life hardly troubled" by the misery it produces. So Sheikh Yassine calls for "concluding a pact of mutual aid among humankind that crosses the boundaries of state structures and goes above the heads of official institutions. [For Islam] this is our ideal of beneficence strictly bound to our ideal of spiritual perfection. This plan for a worldwide humanitarian coalition responds to the utopian dream and the actuality of the flagrant imbalance that rages between north and south."

Similarly, Tariq Ramadan, the leading Muslim intellectual-activist in Europe, together with Nadia Yassine forcefully argues that Muslims and Europeans must move beyond facile denunciations of the United States. Ramadan explains: "To face this reality, we have to speak of the common risks we are facing—not just the Muslim world, but everywhere. It's important to find a way to come to universal values and to say this period is a challenge to all of us together."

We would do well to pay close attention to the words of the Yassines, Ramadan, and other clearly radical—"radical" in its most positive sense—religious figures in the Muslim world. They reveal an Islam fully engaged with the same problems as progressives in the North/West, ready to join coalitions based on similar conceptions of social justice and rights (including gender equality, as demonstrated in this case by the role of Yassine's daughter Nadia as the leader of the largest political movement in Morocco).

Since the famed antiglobalization protests in Seattle in late 1999, it has unfortunately been nearly impossible to get the leadership of the anticorporate globalization movements to even minimally engage Muslims as partners in the struggle for a truly new world order. Whether in Iraq, Pakistan, or Palestine, there are innumerable religious Muslim voices that are progressive and nonviolent, but which are largely ignored by our media and government, as well as, in large measure, NGOs and activists alike. In reality, the more "like us" the Islamist voices I have encountered are—that is, the more they support real democracy, women's rights, tolerance, and real free markets—the more vehemently they reject almost every aspect of the American-dominated globalized order. Why is it, then, that both the American Left and the antiglobalization movement persist in dismissing or outright ignoring these voices and the contributions they might make?

Today's American *Realpolitik* has taken us far from the core ideals that our country was founded on, the kinds of ideals that have inspired Muslims in the universities of Tehran as much as they inspired Catholics in the Gdansk shipyards a generation ago. If we want Muslims to become more like us, perhaps we should become more like the society we claim to be.

If the peace movement and democratic Iraqi forces are to develop a more sophisticated message and strategy and offer a positive alternative discourse to occupation, corruption, and violence, intercommunal solidarity through dialogue and committed nonviolence will be the key mechanisms. This is a daunting challenge, but if relationships can be forged between Iraqis, the larger Arab and Muslim worlds, and activists in the West, the global peace and justice movement may yet gain the upper hand in the struggle against global empire, in Palestine as well as Iraq.

Local Iraqis line up behind piles of gerry cans they hope to fill at a gas station. LYNSEY ADDARIO/CORBIS 2003

BAGHDAD JOURNAL #7

The greeting in Baghdad is "*Assalamu alaykum*," "Peace upon you." One's hand touches one's heart, then reaches out as if making an offering. If you are an American, the greeting will be followed by a generous "Welcome."

I am standing on a dirt street in a poor suburb of Baghdad, a neighborhood of dusty stone walls that shelter boxlike concrete houses. The people who live here have had no running water for seven days; so we've been told by the USAID workers, who are helpless to get them what they need. We've joined the director responsible for the neighborhood to investigate reports that the elderly and babies are dying of dehydration and water-borne illnesses.

The streets are full of children. Sewage runs in rivulets down the ruts of the road and gathers in its craters. The smell is thick, and I try to keep my breathing shallow so as not to inhale it too deeply.

Women have come out of their houses; the younger women are dressed in bright colors and head scarves, the elders in the more traditional black *abeya*. The few men in evidence are older, in their fifties and sixties, and wear the clothes of the conservative religious.

Our guide moves into the crowd. Immediately she is approached by a woman in an *abeya* who has tribal markings on her lower lip and chin. She begins to speak in rapid, forceful Arabic. Our driver, Farouk, translates for me, struggling to keep up with the torrent of words: There is no water, no electricity, sewage in the streets, our children are suffering, can you not see what a disaster this will become? People are dying.

I move closer to the woman to ask a question. She turns to me. Her face lights up with a warm, open smile. "Welcome," she says in English, reaching out her hand. "*Salaam alechem.*"

"Why can't the Americans give us our electricity and water?" she pleads with me in Arabic.

I am reminded of the repeated questions I heard in February: "Why does Mr. Bush want to bomb us?"

I still have no answers to these questions.

Iraqis gather around a water tank provided by the Iran Red Crescent Organization. LYNSEY ADDARIO/CORBIS 2003

EVERY MORNING THE WAR GETS UP FROM SLEEP

Ah! This is Baghdad: I move through it every day, to and fro,
While I squat in this cold exile. I look for it
In the demonstrators who move along Rashid Street carrying banners,
In the strikes of textile workers,
To whom we throw bags of bread and political tracts.
At dawn, carrying paint, we spray the walls with our slogans:
"Down with Dictatorship!"
In the coffeehouses extending along the river on Abu Nawwas,
In the fishermen by the bridge,
In the monument of Jawad Selim which is riddled with bullets,
In Majid's coffeehouse, where the geniuses and informers sip tea,
Where a poet expelled from college gazes at a window
Behind which three Palestinian girls gaze down the street forever.

Ah! Every morning the war gets up from sleep.
So I place it in a poem, make the poem into a boat, which I throw into the Tigris.

This is war, then.

BACK TO BABYLON

Accept and forget difference or desire that separates and leaves us longing or repelled. Why briefly return to play in broken places, to mock the ground, to collect infant shards, coins, fossils, or the familiar empty canisters and casings that glint from poisoned roots in the blackened dust? We make bad ghosts, and are last to know or believe we too will fade, just as our acrid smoke and those strange flakes of skin and strands of hair will, into largely undocumented extinction. Lie down, lie down; sleep is the best thing for being awake. Do as we've always been told and done, no backward glances or second thoughts, leaving sad markers buried in the sand. Sleep now, dream of children with their heads still on, of grandmothers unburdening clotheslines at twilight, of full kettles slow-ticking over twig embers. Ignore boneless, nameless victims that venture out on bitter gravel to claim remains while we rest.

Pay at the window for re-heated, prejudiced incantations. Take them home and enjoy with wide-screen, half-digested, replayed previews of solemn national celebration. Then sleep, by all means; we'll need all the energy we can muster for compiling this generation's abridged anthology of official war stories, highlights of heedless slaughter, to burnish our long and proud imperial tradition. At some point, by virtue of accidentally seeing and listening, we may find ourselves participating in our own rendering. Few of our prey will be left alive enough to water the sun with their modest, time-rubbed repetitions, to rephrase their particular, unifying laws. Our version of events has already made its money back in foreign distribution and pre-sales; all victory deadlines must be met.

It can get so quiet, with or without the dead watching our constant deployments. From our tilted promontory we may see one last woman scuffle away across cracked parchment of dry wash beneath us, muttering to herself—or is she singing at us?—as she rounds the sheared granite face and disappears into a grove of spindly, trembling tamarisk shadows lining the main road. We'll soon hear little other than our breathing, as shale cools and bats rise to feed, taking over from sated swallows. Night anywhere is home, darkness a cue for turning inward, quiet an invitation to review our expensive successes before morning extraction from the twin rivers of our common cradle.

February 2003.

RADIO CORRESPONDENT

I.
At 8 years old
I stood on the equator
beside ant hills that were taller than me
in a game park in post-colonial Kenya
with Mount Kilimanjaro—its clouds
    and snow
shimmering in the distance
as I tried to coax harmony from a goat-
    skinned drum

Masai tribes people had danced in this
    same place
the previous evening
their bare feet
stomping dust
into low clouds
that reddened the sunset
by putting little bits of earth into the sky
and calling the sky and the night
closer to the ground
collapsing the distance
between earth and the stars
between the drum and the sun
between prayer and celebration
between Hollis and the snows of
    Kilimanjaro
and my 8-year-old soul

I never wanted to leave that place
As night fell a symphony of wildlife
flooded my ears
I crawled on top of a small boulder
and strained to touch the sky
I wanted to slip the moon beneath my
    tongue
let constellations trickle down my throat
and sing me closer to the universe

but maybe that would be too much
to swallow

II.
One day your heart will abandon you
Your tongue will not work
And your ears will create their own sounds
The betrayals will no longer be outside
    of you

The world is coming apart
And I'm shitting blood in the Palestine
    Hotel
As other Americans liberate Iraq
With bombs and murder
Photoplay
I want to run to my balcony
And work
But I haven't had
A solid bowel movement
Since I got here
And my system is unravelling
A porcelain throne of blood
Is beneath me

III.
So much chatter
In the sky
Empty streets
No more horns
Bleating warning and permissions
So much dead traffic and language
Allah has retreated into the Euphrates
as Jesus shepherds cluster bombs

There are no new ways
to describe destruction
all that is new

is your fear   blindness and   prayers
invested in the rubble
commingled with the smoke
and licks of flames
the hearts on the ground
and hearts swirling above them
in machines
separated by much more
than airspace
the lean wild dogs
don't run the banks of the Tigris
in the daylight
they stay hidden in the rubble of
bombed-out buildings
hiding like cicadas in the half-built
   promises
unfinished construction
shelter and pause before the gravity
   strikes
at night they run the banks of the river
crooning
aboriginal
inscrutable
as they sing the air raid sirens awake
tax dollars and jet engines make you run
to your balcony
break out your Sony
and attempt thin
and one-dimensional recordings
of the city
Baghdad is unstrung
in a corset of sound
murder and chaos are concussive
they don't just shout in your face
they grab you by the collarbone and

blow into it
the tune is so familiar
you want to leave your skin and your
   body behind
you weak motherfucker
what made you think you could do this
put down your superficial electronics
and be present
the air bends more than it shakes
it will push itself into everyday sounds
car doors closing
dishes breaking
engines backfiring
it will find ways to remain close to you
camouflaged and close
familiar
for all your days

and the shit
hasn't even
really begun

Baghdad 3/21/03

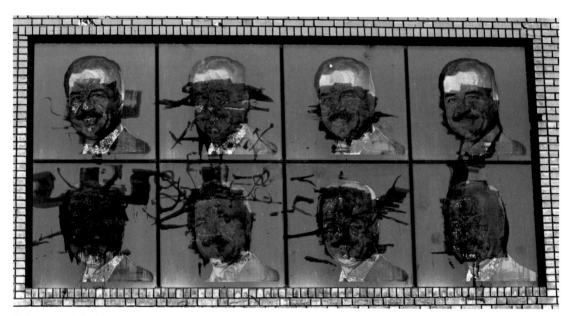

Defaced mural of Saddam Hussein. LYNSEY ADDARIO/CORBIS 2003

CONTRIBUTORS

Lynsey Addario is a photojournalist based in Istanbul, Turkey, where she photographs for the *New York Times*, the *New York Times Magazine*, *Time*, and *Newsweek*, among others, through her New York–based photo agency, Corbis. In January 2003 Lynsey moved her base to Istanbul, in order to situate herself closer to feature and news stories in the Middle East. In February 2003 she traveled to Iraq, where she spent almost seven months covering the war for the *New York Times Magazine*, *Time*, and the *New York Times* newspaper.

Fadhil al-Azzawi was born in Kirkuk, north Iraq, in 1940. He has a BA in English literature from Baghdad University and a PhD in journalism from Leipzig University. He has edited literary magazines and newspapers in Iraq and abroad and has been publishing his work since the 1960s—seven volumes of poetry, eight novels, a collection of short stories, two works of criticism, and numerous translations into Arabic from English and German. His poetry has been translated into many languages, and he is soon to have a major selection of his works published in English by Boa Editions, Ltd. He left Iraq in 1977 and has settled in Germany. He is a consulting editor of *Banipal*.

Medea Benjamin is a powerful and charismatic force in human rights activism. She has struggled for social justice in Asia, Africa, and the Americas for more than twenty years. Benjamin is the founding director of the human rights organization Global Exchange; she also helped form the coalition United for Peace and Justice and is the co-founder of Code Pink: Women for Peace.

Tiosha Bojorquez Chapela was born in Mexico City in 1973. After spending some years in various provinces of Babylon, he returned to Mexico, where he is working as a translator and scriptwriter while finishing one degree in Linguistics from the National School of Anthropology and History (ENA), and another degree in the department of English Literature at the National Autonomous University of Mexico (UNAM).

Kristina Borjesson, an Emmy- and Murrow Award–winning investigative reporter, has worked for CBS and CNN, and she is the author of *Into the Buzzsaw: Leading Journalists Expose the Myth of a Free Press*.

Anne E. Brodsky is Associate Professor of Psychology and Women's Studies at the University of Maryland Baltimore County (UMBC) and author of *With All Our Strength: The Revolutionary Association of the Women of Afghanistan* (Routledge, 2003).

Mike Davis is a MacArthur Fellow and the author of several books, including *Dead Cities*, *City of Quartz*, and *Ecology of Fear*. He lives in San Diego.

Jodie Evans has been a political, environmental, and social activist for more than thirty years, and she is the co-founder of Code Pink: Women for Peace. She visited Iraq in February and July of 2003.

Tahmeena Faryal is a Pakistan-based member of the Revolutionary Association of the Women of Afghanistan (RAWA) and serves on their Foreign Affairs Committee.

Lisa Fredsti is a writer and researcher based in Venice, California. She is currently working on a pop biography of the late Chinese premier Zhou Enlai.

Sandra Fu is a Los Angeles–based freelance writer and a senior editor for Morphizm.com.

Amy Goodman is host of the award-winning nationally syndicated daily grassroots news hour, *Democracy Now!*, broadcasting on public radio/TV stations nationally, and streaming at www.democracynow.org.

Amir Hussain is a member of the Department of Religious Studies at California State University, Northridge (CSUN). His area of research is on the study of Islam, specifically contemporary Muslim societies in North America.

Eman Ahmed Khammas is a journalist. She has written numerous reports on the conditions of occupation in Iraq and is currently the director of Occupation Watch. Khammas lives in Baghdad, is a Sunni Muslim who is married with two children, and speaks ardently for nonviolent means to political change.

Naomi Klein is the author of *No Logo: Taking Aim at the Brand Bullies* and *Fences and Windows: Dispatches from the Front Lines of the Globalization Debate*. She writes an internationally syndicated column for *The Nation* and *The Guardian*.

Mark LeVine's research, activism, and music engage the histories and political and cultural economies of the modern Middle East, Islam, and globalization. He has worked with artists such as Mick Jagger, Ozomatli, Hassan Hakmoun, Dr. John, and Chuck D, and is the author of *Overthrowing Geography: Jaffa, Tel Aviv, and the Struggle for Palestine, 1880–1948* (University of California Press, 2005) and the tentatively titled *Why They Don't Hate Us: From Culture Wars to Culture Jamming in the Age of Globalization*, forthcoming from Oneworld Press.

Yanar Mohammed is the founder of Defense of Iraqi Women's Rights (DIWR), a Toronto-based women's group founded in 1998. After the fall of the Baath Regime, Mohammed went to Baghdad and was a founding member of the Organization of Women's Freedom in Iraq (founded June 22, 2003). She is also the editor in chief of *Al-Mousawat* (Equality) newspaper , a radical defender of women's rights in Iraq.

Viggo Mortensen is a co-editor of this book and founder of Perceval Press. He dedicates the poem "Back to Babylon" to the people of Iraq and the United States of America.
Christian Parenti is the author, most recently, of *The Soft Cage: Surveillance in*

America From Slavery to the War on Terror (Basic, 2003), and is a fellow at City University of New York's Center for Place, Culture, and Politics.

Pilar Perez is an activist, art curator, and co-founder of Perceval Press. She has edited numerous books that combine art, social issues, and politics.

Jerry Quickley's hard-hitting poems and essays are widely anthologized—from New York to Munich, from Bordeaux to Baghdad, he perfects the art of creative revolution. In Iraq as a radio correspondent and documentary filmmaker during the early days of the war, he recently returned to occupied Iraq to complete his documentary project and continue to broadcast independent, unembedded radio reports.

Omid Safi is an assistant professor of Islamic Studies at Colgate University in Hamilton, New York. He specializes in Islamic mysticism, contemporary Islamic thought, and medieval Islamic history. He is a member of the steering committee for the Study of Islam at the American Academy of Religion, the largest international organization devoted to the academic study of religion. He is the author of *Progressive Muslims: On Justice, Gender, and Pluralism* (Oneworld Press, 2003).

Lauren Sandler, a journalist, is investigating issues of women and culture in Iraq for the Carr Foundation.

Joseph Wilson was deputy chief of mission at the U.S. Embassy in Baghdad from 1988 to 1991. In July, he called into question the Bush administration's assertions about Iraq seeking uranium from Africa by revealing that he had been asked by the U.S. government to look into such claims—and had reported in early 2002 that they were unfounded. He is an adjunct scholar at the Middle East Institute in Washington, D.C.

Nadia Yassine was born in 1958 in Casablanca, Morocco. In 1980 she earned a bachelor's degree in political science. She is the author of *Toutes Voiles Dehors* (published in Morocco and France), translated into English as *Raising Full Sail Towards Original Islam* (not yet published). Yassine is a prominent figure of Islamic renaissance, not only in Morocco, but internationally as well. Through interviews with international newspapers, magazines, and TV channels, she has been solicited to expound the viewpoints of her movement, *Jamâtu Al Adl Wal Ihssân* (Justice and Spirituality Association), which is concerned with domestic and foreign issues involving the Muslim world.

Howard Zinn is professor emeritus of Political Science at Boston University and is the author of the best-selling *A People's History of the United States*, and many other books, including *The Zinn Reader* and *Artists in Times of War*.

ORGANIZATIONS

Alternet:
an online magazine created by
the Independent Media Institute
(www.alternet.org).

American Friends Service Committee:
a Quaker organization providing
worldwide peace and justice programs
(www.afsc.org).

Antiwar.com:
a resource site for antiwar news
articles, viewpoints, and activities
(www.antiwar.com).

Baghdad.com:
a World News Network of extensive
resource for news articles and events
(www.baghdad.com).

Baghdad Bulletin:
independent coverage of the
redevelopment of Iraq
(www.baghdadbulletin.com).

Baghdad Independent Media Center:
independent news produced by
Iraqis in Iraq
(www.almuajaha.com).

Bring Them Home:
U.S. military families and veterans
opposed to the occupation (www.
bringthemhomenow.com).

Center for Defense Information:
an independent monitoring agency
of military activity in Iraq (www.cdi.
org).

Code Pink: Women for Peace:
is a women-initiated grassroots
peace and social justice movement that
seeks positive social change through
proactive creative protest and
nonviolent direct action
(www.codepinkalert.org).

Common Dreams:
a cutting-edge website publishing
progressive visions
(www.commondreams.org).

Costs of War:
a running daily count of the
cost of war in Iraq (www.costofwar.
com).

Democracy Now!:
an online website of Amy Goodman's
Pacifica Radio show
(www.democracynow.org).

Electronic Iraq:
an Internet portal of breaking news
from Iraq
(www.electroniciraq.net).

Fairness and Accuracy in Reporting:
a national media watch documenting
media bias and censorship (www.fair.
org).

Fellowship of Reconciliation:
an interfaith organization committed
to international nonviolence (www.
forusa.org).